MIRACLES THROUGH FORGIVENESS

DEACON STEVE GRECO

Copyright © 2019 Deacon Steve Greco

All rights reserved.

ISBN:
978-1090630865

CONTENTS

5

ACKNOWLEDGEMENTS

I want to thank all of those at Spirit Filled Hearts for your prayers and inspiration, especially my loving wife, **Mary Anne Greco**.

I appreciate all of you who have inspired me with your love and stories of forgiveness. I especially want to thank **Jim Graves** who did a great job with his ideas and editing of the book. I also want to thank **Geoff Gudelman** for his graphic design of the cover and the back page.

Finally, I want to thank Bishop **Tim Freyer** for his prayers, support, and writing the forward of the book.

FOREWARD

It is my great pleasure to offer my enthusiastic endorsement for Deacon Steve Greco's 5th book, *Miracles Through Forgiveness*, in which he offers us many important insights into growing closer to Christ through forgiveness. I have known Deacon Steve for many years, and have participated in his conferences, and have twice been on his radio program *Empowered by the Spirit*.

When I was named a bishop, I chose the following Scripture passage as my motto:

> Matthew 28: 19-20 "Go, therefore, and make disciples of all nations, baptizing them in the name of the Father, and of the Son, and of the holy Spirit, teaching them to observe all that I have commanded you. And behold, I am with you always, until the end of the age."

As he relates in his books, as a young man, Deacon Steve had his own personal conversion to Christ. While he was born and raised Catholic,

God's grace touched him in a special way and he resolved to devote himself entirely to his faith and respond affirmatively to the Great Commission. He immersed himself in the Scriptures, and began to share his love for Christ with great joy and enthusiasm among those whom God brought across his path.

He was ordained a deacon for our Roman Catholic Diocese of Orange in 2007, and has since retired from his career in the pharmaceutical industry and devotes himself full time to evangelization. His unique ministry, *Spirit Filled Hearts*, has reached many with its message of Christ's love for His people, devoting oneself to knowing and loving Him most particularly through reception of the sacraments and study of Scripture, and then the taking of that message and, in turn, sharing it with others in our lives.

As a bishop, I have a particular function in the leadership of the Church, celebrating the Sacred Mysteries at the altar, preaching the Gospel and making available the sacraments to the people. While you will easily find me in a chancery office or parish church, where I have more limited access is in the workplace, the home or other public places where there are millions of people in desperate need of Christ's love and forgiveness. That is the vital role of the laity. First, to live a vibrant Catholic life, practicing the Corporal and Spiritual Works of Mercy and living according to the Ten Commandments. Next, as people come to see how our faith transforms us into better people, into images of Christ, then they can look for appropriate opportunities to share the faith and invite others to join us for Mass and other activities at our parishes.

An important component of our efforts to evangelize must be forgiveness. We cannot be effective ambassadors for Christ if we harbor angry or vengeful thoughts. Such animosity will block His grace from entering our hearts and limit its transformative power. Although it may seem difficult, we look to Jesus to give us His grace for while He was being crucified, prayed:

> Luke 23:34 "Father, forgive them, they know not what they do."

Forgiveness is an important part of loving others, and love must be a central part of any efforts to evangelize. Remember, Christ told us:

> John 13:35 "This is how all will know that you are my disciples, if you have love for one another."

I want to congratulate Deacon Steve on his outstanding book. I hope that by following its guidance it will help you embrace forgiveness in your life, experience miracles of grace and bring light into a world that has been so darkened by sin.

Most Reverend **Timothy Freyer**
Auxiliary Bishop of Orange, California

INTRODUCTION

I am blessed! Blessed that God has chosen me to be an instrument of His love and healing. I have been involved in the Lord's ministry for over 40 years. During that time, I have learned more than ever that God wants to provide us with grace upon grace. It is this grace that allows God's love to flow into us and leads to spiritual, mental, emotional and physical healing.

God's miracles are common when we look for them. The Catholic definition of miracles is "God's supernatural intervention in our lives."

When I ask people who attend my talks if they have experienced miracles, more than 90% of them raise their hands. So many people have experienced unexplained things in their lives that are blessings and can only be attributed to God. Many Catholics and Christians have faith that moves mountains. They believe and expect miracles!

However, many people don't realize that one of the greatest miracles they can experience is to heal themselves of the lack of forgiveness in their hearts. The definition of forgiveness is "the action or process

13

of forgiving or being forgiven."

Forgiveness is a state of being. It is a desire to want to have a heart of forgiveness. We must ask for forgiveness and expect that we will receive it. To have a forgiving heart changes everything. To have a forgiving heart is to have the heart of Jesus. If we let it, it transforms us into warriors for Christ.

One of the talks I gave in Northern California on healing reminded me of how many people hold on to bitterness and animosity and have unforgiving hearts. I emphasized that before any of them came up for prayer, they needed to forgive anyone who they hadn't forgiven.

Suddenly there was a huge gasp. It was obvious that many had not forgiven people who had hurt them. Often it was those closest to them: spouses, children, parents, friends, bosses and co-workers. It was those individuals who had the ability to truly penetrate their hearts and minds and hurt them emotionally. When many of them came up for prayer, they asked for the grace to forgive those who had hurt them.

There is a close relationship between healing, forgiveness and miracles. That is the basis of this book. Do you want to receive the miracles that God wants to give you? Most of us are like the characters in a number of the stories in Scripture. Do we really want to be healed of our issues with forgiveness?

I am often reminded of the story in Matthew of the healing of two blind men:

> Matthew 9, 27-29 "And as Jesus passed on from there, two blind men followed [him], crying out, 'Son of David, have pity on us!' When he entered the house, the blind men approached him and Jesus said to them, 'Do you believe that I can do this?' 'Yes, Lord,' they said to him. Then he touched their eyes and said, 'Let it be done for you according to your faith.'"

Jesus wants to forgive and heal you of your lack of forgiveness. Ask God for the grace to forgive those who have hurt you, yourself, and yes, forgive God for not giving you what you think you need. This is often the basis for our drifting away from God and into what the world has to offer. The lies of the world become truth to us.

The miracle of God's forgiveness is that He wants to heal us completely. This includes being healed of past and current wounds. Do you want to be healed? To be filled with the power of the Holy Spirit?

There are obstacles to forgiveness. While there are

many obstacles to this grace, all the challenges can be overcome by the love of Jesus. We must open our hearts to God's love that will enable us to forgive ourselves, others and God. We will examine how God can give us physical healing, inner healing, emotional healing, healing of memories and healing of the family tree.

Understanding mercy and forgiveness will enable us to spread God's love. We have an enemy who does not want us to receive God's mercy and love. Satan and the fallen angels try to prevent a forgiving attitude from entering our hearts and souls. This book will examine spiritual warfare and how the enemy tries to defeat us.

During the journey of this book we will explore faith and forgiveness, family healing, the necessity of the sacraments and their role in forgiveness, the need for endurance and finally living our purpose.

You have been chosen to read and absorb this book so that you may be healed of your lack of forgiveness and to open your heart so that miracles will flow into your heart, soul and lives.

CHAPTER 1
THE OBSTACLES TO FORGIVENESS

To forgive is to open our hearts to God's love. For that reason, it is not easy. The world, the enemy, and our own weakness fight against what we need to receive the love and grace of Jesus. We have often heard the saying, "to err is human and to forgive divine." I am convinced that the spirit of true forgiveness only comes from God.

We often want to forgive those people in our lives who have hurt us, but we feel it is beyond our ability to do so. That is when God must come into our hearts and heal us. Our healing is the miracle we reference. Whether or not you want to call it a miracle, remember that without God we can do nothing. If we don't have the ability to forgive and God's grace enables us to change our attitude and forgive, then, for me, it is God's miracle that has allowed forgiveness in our hearts.

When we don't forgive, the enemy has a field day. Lack of forgiveness is drinking poison and expecting it to harm another person. When we don't forgive, it doesn't hurt anyone but ourselves.

Why is forgiveness so difficult for us? There are many reasons and obstacles that need to be overcome in order to enable the miracle of forgiveness to penetrate our hearts.

The first obstacle is perhaps the most common. We simply don't want to forgive. We justify not forgiving by what has happened to us. One story that was particularly poignant for me occurred on one of my visits to a local jail. I was leading a communion service and delivered a homily on forgiveness. I told them how they were forgiven and how much God wanted us to reflect that forgiveness in our lives by forgiving other people.

One of the women in the jail looked up to me and

said, "How do I forgive my husband? He put me out for prostitution." Tough one to answer. There are many difficult circumstances to answer. So many people have been abused sexually, emotionally and physically. It is gut wrenching to hear.

I answered her in this way: "Yes, that is difficult. That is why we must turn over our lives and surrender to Jesus. Jesus will give us the grace to forgive, even in the most difficult situations. When we don't forgive, we only hurt ourselves." She looked at me and her eyes brightened. She smiled and nodded her head.

Ask yourself this question. Are you justifying your lack of forgiveness? Do you find yourself constantly telling yourself and other people the story about why you aren't able to forgive someone? When we don't forgive we have a hardened heart that blocks the grace and blessings of God.

The second obstacle is that we think we don't have to forgive. I have heard people say it is not necessary to forgive. It is part of their personality and not a big deal. People think that it will

19

weaken us or make us vulnerable to be hurt if we forgive too easily.

There is often a misunderstanding of forgiveness. Many people believe that forgiveness means we must reconcile with those who have wronged us. Or, even worse, they think that we need to condone what has been done to them. Neither is true.

To forgive is to open up our hearts to God's love. It is our ability to extend that love to those who have hurt us. It is not condoning what happened, or forgetting it, but it is not allowing it to harm us. We focus on loving everyone with the love of Jesus.

A third obstacle is that we fail to take responsibility for our behavior. We demand an apology or, even worse, that the person we believe wronged us make some kind of reparation. That is not the attitude for which God is looking.

How often must we forgive? That is the question Peter asked Jesus:

> Matthew 18: 21-22, "Then Peter approaching asked him, 'Lord, if my

brother sins against me, how often must I forgive him? As many as seven times?' Jesus answered, 'I say to you, not seven times but seventy-seven times.'"

In our culture, we are not sure what this means. To the Jews at the time of Jesus, it was obvious what it meant: we are to always forgive. No matter what is happening, we are to forgive. No excuses. It is part of the Lord's Prayer: "Forgive us our trespasses as we forgive those who trespass against us."

When we try to justify our lack of forgiveness we leave an open door for the enemy into our lives. When this happens, the gifts of the Spirit are hindered and our ministry is weakened. The enemy uses the opening of lack of forgiveness to harden our hearts. This can definitely lead to bondage by evil spirits. Often it leads to addiction.

A fourth obstacle is our struggle to forgive ourselves. We will examine this in greater detail in the next chapter. We may think we do not deserve to be forgiven. We punish ourselves for not doing something that we believe we should have done. This is a false pride. Jesus has

21

forgiven us. Who are we to say we shouldn't be forgiven?

There are other obstacles, but these are the major ones. The most important thing is that we are to forgive at all times and in all circumstances. By holding on to our pain and judging others, we bring pain into our lives. Without Jesus in our hearts, it is nearly impossible, if not totally impossible, to forgive. Surrender your heart to Jesus and everything changes. We must forgive because we receive from Jesus that we have been unconditionally forgiven. We say yes to receive and give forgiveness.

CHAPTER 2
FORGIVING YOURSELF

We are forgiven. Amen? We may know that in our heads, but is it in our hearts? How many of us condemn ourselves for what we think we should have done, or mistakes that we have made? That has been my biggest challenge in my life!

Why is life so difficult? I asked my brother Bill that question. His answer? "Because it is supposed to be." What adds to the challenge is that the devil wants us to believe that we are junk. That is one of the reasons I love Marriage Encounter. They have a saying: "God does not make junk!"

I have found that many people have the same challenge I do, a difficulty in forgiving themselves. I grew up in an environment where it felt like I had to be perfect in everything I did. If I wasn't perfect then I wasn't loved, or so I believed. I was condemned or ignored; that is what it felt like.

This is what my life was like. If my behavior was pleasing to my parents, I was accepted and praised. If my behavior was not pleasing, then I was ignored, sent to my room, or, worst case scenario, physically beaten. What did that lead to in my actions? Wanting to be accepted, I led a double life: the life I wanted my parents to see, and my real life. I was not free. I was in bondage.

Jesus told us clearly in John:

> John 10:10 "I came so that they might have life and have it more abundantly."

Yet because I didn't know Jesus on a personal basis, I relied on myself to try to survive emotionally. How did it work out? Not well. I hid my feelings. I only shared what I wanted my parents or other people to know. This was not freedom. I needed to be set free by Jesus Christ.

A few years ago, I met a woman at an SCRC Charismatic Renewal convention in Anaheim who also had this "condemnation of self" syndrome. I saw her after one of my workshops and she told me she needed to talk to me in private. She tracked me down after the Saturday evening service and spoke to me about her life. She had traveled down from the Northwest with her pastor and was very active in her church. However, she was holding on to a secret. She blurted out that no one, including the priests at her parish, knew that she had had an affair.

She looked at me with sad eyes and said, "My life is over. I cheated on my husband. God can never forgive me and I can never forgive myself." Perhaps some of you reading this book feel the same. You have had an affair or worse. Many women have had abortions or children out of wedlock. So much pain. So many sins.

I say to you who are in bondage and pain what I told her: "Who is whispering in your ear that you are not forgiven? It cannot be Jesus! He died on the Cross for your sins. He has forgiven you! He wants you to receive that forgiveness and healing!" She began to cry violently. But it was a healing

25

cry. Her eyes where open to the truth. It was the lies of the devil that she had believed! She realized that she had been set free by the death and resurrection of Jesus Christ! That was a total and complete miracle! Her eyes were opened. The bondage was gone forever!

You have been freed by the same death and resurrection of Our Savior! It is understanding and meditating on this reality that will change your life! So many people are living in bondage. They don't truly believe that when Jesus died and rose again it set them free if they accept this unconditional gift. That is the "Good News of Jesus Christ."

For most of my life I was in bondage. I felt I was garbage. I was never good enough no matter what I did. I kept it a secret. You'd never know that was true. It was well hidden by my double life.

When I was 28 years old I was a district sales manager with a pharmaceutical company. One day I was working with a sales representative in Bakersfield. He was a friend and fellow cradle Catholic. He showed up with a Holy Spirit pin on his suit jacket. My eyes widened and I said,

26

"Catholics don't wear Holy Spirit pins." He looked at me with a big smile on his face and said, "I found Jesus! I discovered Him on a personal basis."

I was stunned. I told him he had Jesus every Sunday in the Mass and Eucharist. He wasn't buying it. He had had a transformation. A "born again" experience. He was totally different. It was obvious that he had peace, was excited and wanted to live a life based upon following Jesus.

I had a long drive home from Bakersfield. I couldn't stop thinking about my life. It looked on the surface that I was a good Catholic Christian. I was involved in many activities in my parish. But I knew differently. If you followed me around I doubt that you could come to a conclusion that I was a solid and devout follower of Jesus. My behavior outside of church, my conversations, my actions and thoughts were not someone who had surrendered his life to Jesus.

I couldn't stop thinking about it. I felt like a phony. I knew the truth. It didn't matter what others thought of me. I didn't know what to do.

27

When I got home, my wife was gone and I was alone. I made a decision that changed my life forever. I now call it "fervent prayer." Praying from the heart. That is why our ministry is named "Spirit Filled Hearts." You can fool yourself in thinking something in your head, but your heart is reality. I thought of the good thief on the cross, the centurion, the tax collectors in the Bible and all the saints who were totally committed to Jesus.

I was in my bedroom. I looked intensely into my eyes in the mirror on my closet door and said this prayer from the heart, "Lord Jesus, I give you my life, no matter the cost. Take over my life completely and use me to do your will." I meant it. You can't fake it if you truly mean it! Try it now! You won't believe how wonderful it will be!

Suddenly, my life changed. I went into the living room and saw this big white book on the table with lots of pictures in it. It was dusty and unopened. Yes, you guessed it, it was the Bible! I started reading it and I couldn't believe what it contained!

The words leapt off the pages at me. It was like I never heard or read them before.

> John 3:16 "For God so loved the world that he gave his only Son, so that everyone who believes in him might not perish but might have eternal life."

Wow! Jesus died for me personally! Somehow, it penetrated my heart for the first time. I got really excited. I kept reading and I couldn't put the book down. My wife tells me that I was reading Scripture 6-8 hours a day for weeks and weeks.

I turned to the eighth chapter of Romans.

> Romans 8:1 "Hence, now there is no condemnation for those who are in Christ Jesus."

Wow again! This verse transformed me. I had been condemning myself my whole life. I was never good enough. I felt unworthy. Dirty. Not filled with hope or joy but with shame and remorse. Suddenly, everything changed. I was crying, filled with joy. When you surrender to the love of Jesus, who died for us personally, you will be truly free.

I kept reading the eighth chapter of Romans.

Romans 8: 14-17 "For those who are led by the Spirit of God are children of God. For you did not receive a spirit of slavery to fall back into fear, but you received a spirit of adoption, through which we cry, '*Abba*, Father!' The Spirit itself bears witness with our spirit that we are children of God, and if children, then heirs, heirs of God and joint heirs with Christ, if only we suffer with him so that we may also be glorified with him."

Wow! Think about it. When we give our lives to Jesus we are children of God. We no longer are slaves. No more fear. We are adopted children of God. We will be with Jesus forever. Suddenly the reality of these truths penetrated me at my very core. I felt like a veil had been removed from me.

2 Corinthians 3: 16-18 "But whenever a person turns to the Lord the veil is removed. Now the Lord is the Spirit, and where the Spirit of the Lord is, there is freedom. All of us, gazing with unveiled face on the glory of the Lord, are being transformed into the same image from glory to glory, as from the Lord who is

30

the Spirit."

The words leapt off the page at me. My eyes were opened regarding who I truly was, how much God loved me, and what I was to do with my life. But there was much more.

I read further.

> Romans 8:28 "We know that all things work for good for those who love God."

I now truly loved God. No matter what, God will make things work for good. I read on.

> Romans 8:35, 38-39 "What will separate us from the love of Christ? Will anguish, or distress, or persecution or famine, or nakedness or the sword? For I am convinced that neither death, nor life, nor angels, nor principalities, nor present things, nor future things, nor powers, nor height, nor depth, nor any other creature will be able to separate us from the love of God in Christ Jesus our Lord."

This was fantastic but so different for me, because I had known only conditional love.

31

I kept reading.

> Ephesians 1:3-8 "Blessed be the God and Father of our Lord Jesus Christ, who has blessed us in Christ with every spiritual blessing in the heavens, as he chose us in him, before the foundation of the world, to be holy and without blemish before him. In love he destined us for adoption to himself through Jesus Christ in accord with the favor of his will for the praise of the glory of his grace that he granted us in the beloved.
>
> "In him, we have redemption by his blood, the forgiveness of transgressions, in accord with the riches of his grace that he lavished upon us."

I couldn't believe what I was reading. I was blessed with every spiritual blessing? What did that mean? Could that really be true? In my heart, I knew it was true! I was chosen to be holy? Incredible! I was His adopted son? Phenomenal! My sins were forgiven? I was frozen. How come I didn't know this?

I was so excited that I couldn't stop talking about these verses and how much Jesus loved us. Everywhere I went, no matter who it was, I was telling them about these verses and more. I memorized them and spoke to my wife, brothers, parents and friends. Everyone, all the time.

On Super Bowl Sunday, I went to a party. I was dipping a chip at the same time another man was doing the same. I looked up and asked him, "Do you know Jesus on a personal level?" Somehow, I shouldn't have been surprised: I wasn't invited back to this party or any other!

Soon after that event, I got a phone call from my mother. "Steven, I need to see you as soon as possible." I knew I was in trouble when she called me "Steven." She lived in Glendale, about an hour away. I headed up to see her.

She sat me down in her living room. She was standing. She said, "Tell me the truth. You have joined a cult. No Catholic quotes Scripture and talks about Jesus all the time."

I smiled and said, "Mom, I am more Catholic than ever. I am going to Mass during the week, to confession frequently and following Catholic teaching." My mother wasn't convinced. At any point I felt she would ask me what color Kool-Aid I was drinking!

She looked at me and said, "Please see our cousin the priest at the University of San Diego." I agreed and headed down there the following week. The priest listened intently and said that I was fine but "perhaps you could read some books on the saints."

What is the significance of this story? For the first time I felt loved unconditionally. At no time in my life had I felt that from anyone. I knew that God was real, Jesus was real, and that I was His adopted son.

Yes, I forgave myself for the first time for not being perfect. I no longer condemned myself because Jesus did not condemn me but loved me despite my sins and failures.

I was so excited that my entire life changed. Loving God and serving Him became my priority and gave me joy that I never had before.

My brothers and sisters, Jesus is real. He died for

34

your sins and rose again. He doesn't condemn you so why should you condemn yourself?

It is, indeed, a miracle! God's supernatural intervention has made you free. Forgive yourself now and forever!

CHAPTER 3
FORGIVENESS OF OTHER PEOPLE

I once thought that I didn't have a problem with forgiving other people. I was like the Pharisee who was thankful he wasn't like the tax collector. The Lord asked me to pray and open my heart for Him to reveal to me my true heart of forgiveness.

I was shocked as the Lord revealed to me the seemingly countless number of people I haven't forgiven. I had buried them in the depths of my mind but had never forgiven them. One of the people I hadn't forgiven was my father. Perhaps you also have someone you haven't forgiven, such as a parent, friend or co-worker.

My father grew up during the Depression. He was one of 11 children who had had a difficult life. At a young age, I had difficulty with my speech. He would make fun of me in front of other people. They would laugh at me. I had deep wounds and emotional scars.

As I grew up, my father was distant to me. If my mother was upset with me, she would call my father and he would come storming home from work and head to my room to beat me. To say that was emotionally scarring is an understatement.

Yet I knew he felt he was doing the right thing in his mind. For years I resented him with an unforgiving attitude. Later in his life, I forgave him, and was at his side for years when he was bedridden. It was not easy, but turning to God and asking Him for the grace to forgive my father was the miracle that changed me forever!

One of the most impactful lessons for me was when Pope Saint John Paul II forgave his would-be assassin Mehmet Ali Agca in prison. On May 13, 1981, the pope was crossing St Peter's Square in Vatican City when an attempt was made on his life. Four shots were fired directly at him with a 9-millimeter pistol. The bullets struck the pontiff's lower intestine, right arm and left index finger. He was rushed to the hospital.

The pontiff, with severe blood loss, asked for all Catholics to pray for the man who had shot him. He told the world that he had "sincerely forgiven" Mehmet Ali Agca. I remember thinking: what would I do? How forgiving would I be?

Saint John Paul II followed up with an incredible visit to his would-be assassin in prison. He spoke to him privately, loving him, with the forgiveness of Christ. Demonstrating that it was not just a one-time event, the pope stayed in touch with him and his family. He even requested in 2000 that he be released from prison, which was granted.

After Mehmet Ali Agca was deported to Turkey, in a miracle of Christ's love, personified by Pope Saint John Paul II, he converted to Christianity in 2010! What love! What an example by Pope Saint John Paul II!

Forgiving other people is incredibly difficult. We may have the right intentions but often fail miserably. It reminds me of the Parable of the Sower:

> Matthew 13 18-23 "Hear then the parable of the sower. The seed sown on the path

is the one who hears the word of the kingdom without understanding it, and the evil one comes and steals away what was sown in his heart. The seed sown on rocky ground is the one who hears the word and receives it at once with joy. But he has no roots and lasts only for a time. When some tribulation or persecution comes because of the word, he immediately falls away. The seed sown among the thorns is the one who hears the word, but then worldly anxiety and the lure of riches choke the word and it bears no fruit. But the seed sown on rich soil is the one who hears the word and understands it, who indeed bears fruit and yields a hundred or sixty or thirtyfold."

How does this relate to forgiveness? We start out by wanting to forgive but the enemy whispers in our ears not to do so because of all the things done to you. Our thoughts remind us of what appears to be a major injustice. Perhaps we go further and start to forgive but the person doesn't act as we think they should, we are persecuted by them and then go back to not forgiving.

However, if we stay the course, the grace of God and the many miracles He has in store for us is manifested.

I believe that we are tested in order to grow in holiness when it comes to forgiveness. One of the most difficult challenges of forgiveness to me occurred when I was senior vice president of sales for Bristol-Myers Squibb. I was responsible for 4,000 people and seven billion in sales. I was told that I was a "corporate treasure." I was honored by executives as being one of the top leaders in the company. Then suddenly it all changed. A new CEO was hired and I was seen as expendable. After being a corporate hero I was now not needed. I was called in to my boss's office and fired.

I was in shock. Sales were great. I was beloved by nearly every one. I couldn't understand it. I felt God's hand was in it but it was painful beyond words. How could I forgive those who had fired me? I prayed and asked for strength, faith and the spirit of forgiveness. At first, all I could think of was the Scripture from Deuteronomy 32:35, "Vengeance is mine." I remember thinking and praying, "I turn them over to you for your vengeance for what happened to me." Pathetic, but that is where I was emotionally.

The Lord worked on me and I realized I had to do a lot more. My lack of forgiveness was hurting me spiritually and blocking the grace that Christ wanted to give me. I prayed fervently for the ability to forgive the people who hurt me. The Lord told me I had to love them with His love. I felt it was impossible. What changed was receiving grace and the miracle of Jesus forgiving me.

The Lord told me to see them through His eyes. When I prayed for that to occur I totally changed my attitude. However, the Lord was not done healing me. He then told me again to love them with His love. I closed my eyes and felt the pain and resentment melting away. Is it easy? No! It is not supposed to be easy. It is running the race toward heaven and the crown of life!

When we recognize that we are sinners and don't deserve to be saved or forgiven everything changes. We truly become ambassadors for Christ when we let His forgiveness flow through us. This greatly opens us up to spiritual growth. In my experience, it is a critical step toward holiness.

41

There is a story about an 86-year-old priest who was captured and was to be executed. He asked the guard to untie his hands so that he could bless him and those who were going to execute him. The guard began to mock and ridicule him. The soldier then decided to cut off his hands so that he couldn't bless anyone. After he mutilated the priest, this holy man still blessed all those who were there before he was killed.

When people hurt us, especially emotionally, we are at a crossroad. Do we attempt to do harm in the same way we are hurt or do we try to forgive through the power the Holy Spirit? When we attempt to see the person through the eyes of Jesus, our attitude changes. To Jesus, every person has value. God hates the sin but loves the sinner. We are to do the same. Everyone is made in the image and likeness of God. Jesus died for that person exactly the way he is. Who are we to judge and condemn him?

Jesus is very clear that we need to love our brothers and sisters.

> 1 John 2:10-11 "Whoever loves his brother remains in the light and there is nothing in him to cause a fall. Whoever

OVERCOMING ADVERSITY THROUGH MIRACLES

hates his brother is in darkness; he walks
in darkness and does not know where he
is going because the darkness has blinded
his eyes."

Throughout this powerful letter Saint John tells us
to love one another no matter what.

1 John 4: 7, 11-12 "Beloved, let us love
one another, because love is of God;
everyone who loves is begotten by God
and knows God. Beloved, if God so
loved us, we also must love one another.
No one has ever seen God. Yet, if we
love one another, God remains in us, and
his love is brought to perfection in us."

Notice it doesn't say to love one another if they
treat us well and are nice to us. It doesn't say that
if they earned our love, then it is okay to love
people. No, it is not conditional. No matter how
much they are nice to us or hurt us, we are to
respond to them with the same amount of love!

Is that easy? Of course not! That is why we must
ask for the gift of greater love and forgiveness. It
is a spiritual blessing! The good news? We are
told in the first chapter of Ephesians that we have

received "every spiritual blessing in the heavens." When we love with the love of Jesus we are filled with grace upon grace that is reflected in the first chapter of the Gospel of John. Rejoice! You are chosen to be holy and blessed!

One of the most important things you can do when you are trying to find the grace to forgive is to receive the Sacrament of Reconciliation. It is unfortunate that many people don't understand the grace and power associated with this critical sacrament. Often we are under spiritual attack with a spirit of lack of forgiveness. We have a hardened heart that prevents us from seeing another person as a child of God.

When we go to Reconciliation it is important to confess any grudges, hatred, animosity or any ill will we have toward another person. Often our spirit has been hardened so that we need this sacrament to be set free. Penance is necessary to free us from this sin. Will we be set free immediately? Sometimes, but often we need frequent Reconciliation and daily or frequent Communion to be set free

To be set free is to see things differently. It is important that we make the first step toward the person with whom we are having difficulty in our lives. Try to approach him and let him know your feelings and ask forgiveness if you have done anything to contribute to the problem between the two of you.

In every situation there are two kinds of people who are involved in a conflict with another person. They are the individual who apologizes and the one who does not. If someone apologizes to you it is important that you accept his apology.

> Luke 17:4 "And if he wrongs you seven times in one day and returns to you seven times saying, 'I am sorry,' you should forgive him."

To forgive another person is an act of love, courtesy, charity and is both moral and spiritual. We are told clearly to love our enemies.

> Luke 6:27-30 "But to you who hear I say, love your enemies, do good to those who hate you, bless those who curse you, pray for those who mistreat you. To the person who strikes you on one cheek, offer the other one as well, and from the person who takes your cloak, do not

withhold even your tunic. Give to everyone who asks of you, and from the one who takes what is yours do not demand it back."

There are principles that can help you in your pursuit of forgiveness of others. First, it is important to hate the sin and love the sinner. If someone has sinned against you, then disdain the behavior but love the person and let him know he is loved by you. We see in the eighth chapter of John that Jesus may have been writing the sins of those who wanted to stone the woman in adultery. Remember Jesus tells the woman to "sin no more" but does not condemn her. Neither should you condemn the person who has harmed you.

Luke 6:37-38 "Stop judging and you will not be judged. Stop condemning and you will not be condemned. Forgive and you will be forgiven. Give and gifts will be given to you; a good measure packed together, shaken down, and overflowing, will be poured into your lap. For the measure with which you measure will be in turn be measured out to you."

Second, understand the difference between loving

and liking a person. It is critical that we love with the love of Christ, but we don't have to like the person and be "friends" with him. To like a person often involves an emotional connection. That is not necessary. Don't feel guilty if you don't like the person. Do your best to see them through the eyes of God. He sees them as His child that He created for good. He wants them to have an abundant life in which they turn their heart and soul over to Him. What is necessary is to understand that Jesus died for that person and he is made in the image of God. See him as precious in the eyes of God.

Third, love them with agape love. That is loving them unconditionally and wanting good for the person. Your desire must be that the person be saved and with God forever. You pray for the person to find a deeper relationship with Jesus.

Fourth, move from resentment to no resentment. Under no circumstances are you to try to "get even." You are never to try to get vindictive justice. It is acceptable to have remedial justice to keep the person from hurting others and protect society.

Forgiving other people and loving them with the

love of Jesus takes a tremendous amount of grace. We must pray daily and expect God to act. It is through faith that miracles will happen with your relationships and in your life.

CHAPTER 4
FORGIVING GOD

We know from Scripture that we are to love God totally and unconditionally.

> Matthew 22: 37 "You shall love the Lord, your God, with all your heart, with all your soul, and with all your mind."

Easy right? No! It is not easy. We need grace in order to do it because often our expectations, prayers and desires are not met to our liking.

Not forgiving God is very common. It is just not talked about very much. If a child dies or is very ill, we lose our jobs, get an illness which is severe or for many other reasons, we find ourselves questioning the love of God.

In the Psalms, King David often cries out in anguish to God, questioning why he is being treated the way he is.

Psalm 22:2-3

"My God, my God, why have you abandoned me?

Why so far from my call for help,

from my cries of anguish?

My God, I call by day, but you do not answer;

by night, but I have no relief."

Have you felt abandoned by God? Perhaps you stop going to church as frequently or entirely, or you give up on ministry or even prayer itself. You might feel as David felt in Psalm 35.

Psalm 35:17 "O Lord, how long will you look on?

Restore my soul from their destruction,

my very life from lions!"

David in Psalm 42:10 exclaimed what many at times feel in their lives: "Why do you forget me?"

It is embarrassing to tell people you are angry at God, especially if you are seen as a Christian, or worse yet, are a member of the clergy. For me, I have experienced moments when I couldn't understand why God was allowing things to happen. I was reminded by the Lord of Isaiah:

> Isaiah 55:9 "For as the heavens are higher than the earth,
>
> so are my ways higher than your ways,
>
> my thoughts higher than your thoughts."

In other words, we don't get it. We are not God. Don't try to figure it out because we can't see the big picture. That is where trusting in the Lord must come in. "Jesus, I trust in you!" So many people try to figure out everything. They think they understand but none of us have the mind of God.

Our goal is to be in the presence of the Lord. When that happens, great miracles happen in your life.

John 15:7 "If you remain in me and my words remain in you, ask for whatever you want and it will be done for you."

When that happens you have the peace that only God can give. The challenge is when things don't go the way you want. We have a decision to make on whether or not we want to trust in the Lord.

I constantly try to reflect on my trust and love of the Lord. It is easy when things are going well. For me, one of the great challenges in my life occurred in February 2015. I received a phone call from my daughter saying that she had been in a major accident. It was a day of snow and my daughter Laura had taken her son to go skiing. On returning home, she noticed a car in her lane headed to hit her car head on. She honked repeatedly and the woman driving the other car didn't pay attention for she was on her phone, probably texting. Finally, my daughter was convinced she was going to be hit so she drove into the other lane and went into a snow bank. Unfortunately, the other car went into the other lane also and broad sided my daughter's car. If her husband or other son had been in the car they probably would have been killed.

Both my daughter and my grandson had concussions. They went to the local hospital and had MRI's. My daughter's MRI included her lungs. That is when her life, and that of her family, and my life and my wife's, changed dramatically.

They noticed a tumor in her lungs, but the doctor said it was "probably nothing." They suggested it get checked out. That is when the unspeakable was found: lung cancer! Incredible! She had never smoked, nor even drink alcohol. At age 40, she was in the prime of her life, with two small children ages six and two, and she was diagnosed with this deadly disease!

I started questioning God's love of me. How could this happen to my only daughter? I was in disbelief. I felt that God let me down. I couldn't understand it. I traveled all over preaching God's love but didn't feel it was being returned to me.

It got much worse a few months later. My daughter called me when I was in a meeting in Northern California. I went outside to take the call and heard her say, "The cancer entered my heart and they don't expect me to last the night. I wanted to tell you thank you for being my father and goodbye." Goodbye? Are you kidding? It was a nightmare!

I don't remember what I said, just that I was immediately going to go back to New York, where she lived. I hung up and started lamenting, angry at how God could do this to me and my family. I reached out to God in despair. I didn't know what to do. I questioned God's love of me and my family.

I felt God's response immediately. He told me that He loved my daughter more than I could ever know and imagine. That my Laura was His. I repented of my disbelief and asked forgiveness. I started to praise God for being the God of mercy and forgiveness.

I flew home and my wife and I started to fervently praise and thank God for being the God of healing. We got on a red-eye to JFK in New York and arrived early in the morning. My daughter was at Albany Medical Center. We took the horrible ride to Albany to see her. We were praising God and not talking much.

When we finally arrived at the hospital it took us some time to find my daughter. We finally located her and went to her floor. We found her in the hall. When she saw us she had a big smile on her face. She exclaimed to us, "They misdiagnosed me!" The cancer had not spread. She still had lung cancer but she was not going to die anytime soon. Praise God!

I told my daughter soon after to "make it count." She definitely has done that. Her passion is to dramatically increase lung cancer research. She works with the Department of Defense and a number of pharmaceutical companies to increase awareness of the need for lung cancer research. She is successful and has even started a nonprofit.

I realized that God did know best but part of me still was disappointed. This disappointment also occurred with my daughter-in-law prior to my daughter's illness. She and my son seemed to be so happy and full of life. While pregnant with our first grandchild, she began to have symptoms of pain in her joints. She went to her doctor and they ran many tests. We couldn't believe the result. She had multiple sclerosis! Unbelievable!

I remember driving to the hospital and thinking "give me the disease and take it away from my daughter-in-law." It is so hard to see your children and their families suffer. Why does it happen? We can't understand God's plan. We need to have faith and trust.

Examine yourself and your feelings toward God. Are you holding back from giving more of your time, talent and treasure to God because He has disappointed you? It is important to reflect on your relationship with God. Trust in Him and great miracles will flow into your life!

CHAPTER 5
HEALING THROUGH FORGIVENESS

God is good! All the time! The love of Jesus is far beyond anything we can imagine. During His ministry, Jesus always taught forgiveness.

> Matthew 18:21-22 "Then Peter approaching asked him, 'Lord if my brother sins against me, how often must I forgive him? As many as seven times?' Jesus answered, 'I say to you, not seven times but seventy-seven times.'"

What happens when we don't forgive? It is a poison to our body, soul and spirit. It causes mental and physical problems. If we only understood that God died for our sins, our brokenness and our lack of compassion and forgiveness!

Isaiah 53: 4-5 "Yet it was our pain that he bore,

our sufferings he endured.

We thought of him as stricken,

struck down by God and afflicted,

But he was pierced for our sins,

crushed for our iniquity.

He bore the punishment that makes us whole,

by his wounds we were healed."

By His wounds we are made whole! Whatever hurt we have from other people, our brokenness and pain is there for Jesus to heal. We have to do our part and trust Him. Ask to be healed and want to be healed.

When it comes to healing, I have always felt that the story of the healing of two blind men in Matthew is a great lesson for us.

Matthew 9:27-29 "And as Jesus passed on from there, two blind men followed [him], crying out, 'Son of David, have pity on us!' When he entered the house, the blind men approached him and Jesus said to them, 'Do you believe that I can do this?' 'Yes, Lord' they said to him. Then he touched their eyes and said, 'Let it be done for you according to your faith.'"

Apply this lesson to the miracle of forgiveness. So many times we feel that we don't have it in us to forgive. We are so hurt, and in so much pain, we don't want to forgive or feel it is impossible. We must believe and have faith that God will give us the grace to forgive even when we don't want to or feel like it.

The foundation of all healing is love. The foundation of forgiveness is love. Since God is love, it is not difficult to ascertain that only through God's love flowing into and through us that the miracle of forgiveness can occur.

In order to receive the love of God we must surrender to it. That is so hard for so many people. Where are you on surrendering to the love of God? Is it wishful thinking? One way to test yourself on your willingness to surrender is how you pray. For most people, their prayers are those of petition. Fix this, and do this and that. God becomes like a Santa Claus. We want Him to do what we think will help us, our family, health, finances, etc.

When we surrender to God's love, everything changes. Our petitions become fewer. Our prayers are more praise and worship, wanting to adore Him and do His will. We want the gifts of the Holy Spirit not for ourselves but to build up God's kingdom. We want to be used for healing and to evangelize to help people know Jesus and how much they are loved by Him.

We ask for the power of the Holy Spirit to be the ambassador of Christ.

> Acts 1:8 "But you will receive power when the holy Spirit comes upon you, and you will be my witnesses in Jerusalem, throughout Judea and Samaria, and to the ends of the earth."

When we receive this power we don't want to hate or hold onto ill feelings, but to forgive.

To be healed is to die to our flesh. It is to seek

holiness from our very souls. One of the greatest teachings for us comes from the Beatitudes. To be healed of our lack of forgiveness and receive the miracle of God's love, we must live out the truth of what Jesus is teaching us through the Beatitudes.

Matthew 5:3 "Blessed are the poor in spirit,

for theirs is the kingdom of heaven."

To be poor in spirit is to make God the priority in our lives. If God is the priority, we die to our self. We aren't focused on what others have done to us but how we can love them with the love of God.

The second Beatitude is:

Matthew 5:4 "Blessed are they who mourn,

for they will be comforted."

So many times when we have friction between people, it is because they are hurting regarding something in their lives. It is hard to express our inner feelings when we are hurting. When someone expresses something that is a trigger, we respond negatively. Instead of responding in kind, pray for them and let God lead you in what to say and how to comfort them.

One of the most important verses in Scripture is:

> Matthew 5:6, "Blessed are they who hunger and thirst for righteousness,
>
> for they will be satisfied."

Think about it. When we focus on doing the will of the Father, which is what this verse means, we don't have the need to hold onto our animosity. It is impossible to hate, to hold grudges, to have ill will when we are filled with the love of God. When we hunger for it, we will receive it and the Holy Spirit.

> Luke 11:9-13 "And I tell you, ask and you will receive; seek and you will find; knock and the door will be opened to you. For everyone who asks, receives; and the one who seeks, finds; and to the one who knocks, the door will be opened. What father among you would hand his son a snake when he asks for a fish? Or hand him a scorpion when he asks for an egg? If you then, who are wicked, know how

to give good gifts to your children, how much more will the Father in heaven give the holy Spirit to those who ask him?"

When we seek God with all our heart, soul, mind and strength, everything changes.

Mercy always is a key component of forgiveness.

Matthew 7:7 "Blessed are the merciful,

for they will be shown mercy."

We will cover this in greater detail in a later chapter, but our ability to be merciful means that we forgive those who hurt us through the gift of mercy. We will receive mercy from the Lord to a greater extent when we are merciful.

One aspect of being clean of heart means that we focus on God and not on our hurts.

Matthew 5:8, "Blessed are the clean of heart,

for they will see God."

When we have ill will and don't forgive, it means that our focus is not on God. We are not having God as our priority but our hurt.

To be a peacemaker means we are living the peace that only God can provide.

> John 14:27 "Peace I leave you, my peace I give to you. Not as the world gives do I give it to you. Do not let your hearts be troubled or afraid."

When we have that peace we can truly be a peacemaker and a child of God.

> Matthew 5:9 "Blessed are the peacemakers,
>
> for they will be called children of God."

You can't give what you don't have. How can you give peace to others unless you are connected to God?

> John 15:5 "I am the vine, you are the branches. Whoever remains in me and I in him will bear much fruit, because without me you can do nothing."

Read this over and over. Without me you can do nothing. You can't forgive. You can't be healed. You can't have an abundant life.

The eighth Beatitude focuses on being persecuted

for living our faith in Jesus.

> Matthew 5:10 "Blessed are they who are persecuted for the sake of righteousness, for theirs is the kingdom of heaven."

I believe that if we aren't persecuted, then we are not fully living out our faith. Often we are ridiculed and persecuted because of what we believe in. If we believe in life and not abortion, then according to many people we are not in step with today's world. Or, we may be persecuted for believing that a marriage is between one man and one woman.

The question for us is: how do we respond when we are under attack? Do we reply in kind? Show lack of forgiveness? Get angry? Or do we reflect the patience of the Lord? It is difficult not to be upset when we are ridiculed or made fun of by someone. Yet, we are to not respond in the same way but reflect the love and peace of Jesus.

We also receive healing through the sacraments. We confess our struggle with forgiveness in the Sacrament of Reconciliation. We receive the Eucharist, the Body and Blood of Christ, as often as we can. The more I am close to Christ as a result of the sacraments, the less I am focused on my hurts and the more forgiving I can be. Eucharistic adoration is also helpful. Try to go to adoration as often as you can and your heart will definitely soften.

A key component of being healed and forgiveness is to help others in their pursuit of God. We pray over those who are hurting spiritually, mentally, emotionally and physically. It is amazing how the Holy Spirit flows when I am allowing the love of Jesus to flow through me. I have known for a long time that I am being healed when I minister to other people and love them in the way that Jesus wants to love them.

One of the most important lessons for us that dramatically helps with our struggle with the flesh and lack of forgiveness is in Matthew:

> Matthew 25: 34-40 "Then the king will say to those on his right, 'Come you who are blessed by my Father, inherit the kingdom prepared for you from the foundation of the world. For I was hungry and you gave me food, I was thirsty and you gave me drink, a stranger and you welcomed me, naked and you

clothed me, ill and you cared for me, in prison and you visited me.' Then the righteous will answer him and say, 'Lord when did we see you hungry and feed you, or thirty and give you drink? When did we see you naked and clothe you? When did we see you ill or in prison and visit you?' And the king will say to them in reply, 'Amen, I say to you, whatever you did for one of these least brothers of mine, you did for me.'"

Everything changes when we focus on loving our neighbor with the love of Jesus. Like everyone, I have struggled with forgiveness. However, when I minister to the poor, visit those in hospitals, go to prisons and love those who so need the love of Jesus, I feel the love of Christ and the lack of forgiveness is gone. The more I serve others, the more I am healed. The more I die to myself, the more I am a slave to Christ, which is what I so desire!

Another important aspect of being healed of our emotional wounds is to pray for those who have hurt us or those who also struggle to forgive. We know from James:

> James 5:16, "Pray for one another that
> you may be healed. The fervent prayer of
> a righteous person is very powerful."

When we pray for another person, we are healed. We are to be "watchmen" for one another.

One of the most powerful and dramatic examples of this occurred during one of my communion services at a local jail. At the end of the service I had the inmates come up for individual prayer. I asked them what they wanted me to pray for. One woman looked at me intently and said, "I want to pray for my 'bunkie' who has no one to pray for her."

Such love! I was mesmerized by such tremendous love. I am sure that whatever animosity in the heart of the woman asking for prayer was lessened or eliminated by her heartfelt desire and prayer. There is no doubt that love heals. When we pray and love others we are healed.

A great way to be healed of our struggle with forgiveness is to turn to the Blessed Mother. Let her love and her Immaculate Heart change everything. Our spiritual mother wants to teach us how to forgive ourselves and others. Try to pray a decade of the rosary for the people with whom you have issues and lack of forgiveness. I 100% guarantee that your heart will change toward the person.

Another aspect of forgiveness is to be thankful. Think about the people with whom you are struggling. It might be someone at work, such as boss or a co-worker who is driving you crazy. I see this often. People get so many illnesses because of work relationships. They get depressed, have physical sickness and don't know what to do.

Pray for them and let God give you grace to love them. What will really change and heal you is when you thank God for bringing them into your life. What? Impossible? Another way of looking at it is that God wants to teach us how to forgive and how to "love our enemies." Most of the time those people whom we think are enemies don't see themselves as enemies to us. They might not even realize that they are driving us crazy. Begin to love them and thank God they are in your life.

I had a boss who drove me crazy. Whatever I did seemed to be wrong. It felt like I was criticized nonstop. I had a lot of feeling in my heart toward my boss, and none of it was good. What changed? I began to appreciate that my boss wanted me to be better and more effective at my job. When I was thankful to God for my boss, everything changed. I was promoted and recognized in the company. My boss and I respected each other and became friends. If you had experienced the relationship when it wasn't good, you would realize how the relationship developed was truly a miracle!

I believe passionately that forgiveness of others occurs when we are healed of our own wounds. In order for that to happen we need to turn to the love and healing of Jesus. When we are healed we see everything differently. We begin to live the abundant life that Jesus promised us.

CHAPTER 6
FORGIVENESS THROUGH
INNER HEALING

We are emotional beings. No matter how much we try to bury them, our emotions find a way of surfacing. We need healing in order to not have animosity and a lack of forgiveness in our lives. What is healing? It is the process of spiritual, intellectual, emotional and physical restoration under the guidance of the Holy Spirit. In this chapter we will focus on emotional forgiveness.

The need for emotional forgiveness can occur in many ways. It can be from childhood, school, friends, love relationships, work and a variety of situations. It often occurs in our relationships with our parents. That was true for me.

My father was one of 11 children. He believed in being a good provider. Children were to be seen and not heard. In fact, he usually ate alone. If we were there, we were forbidden to talk.

I was active in school, specifically with sports and in student government. There were a number of events that my parents were invited to attend. Often neither of them attended. My mother occasionally showed up, but I can never remember my father coming to any sporting or school event other than my graduation.

What did that do for me? It made me feel that I wasn't worth anything. Everything else was more important than me. It led to my seeking attention from the opposite sex and in general, addictive behaviors, particularly overeating. I have had some degree of depression for as long as I can remember. I always felt that I wasn't good enough. Whatever I did, it was never enough to "fill my bucket."

I was driven. It expressed itself in performance of some kind. In college, it was a high grade average. Later, it was climbing the corporate ladder. I was always trying to win the approval of my parents, especially my father. Nothing seemed to work, no matter what I achieved.

It wasn't until I discovered the love of my Father in heaven that I was on the road to healing. Growing up, my relationship with God the Father was close to zero. I equated Him to my earthly father. Therefore, it was too painful to deal with Him or to try to have a relationship. I never prayed to Him because I felt I wasn't good enough for Him to listen to my requests or needs.

Everything changed when I gave my heart and soul to Jesus Christ. My eyes were opened to unconditional love. Previously, I didn't have a clue to what that was. Love to me was based on performance or what one could do to please another person. When I read Romans, everything changed:

> Romans 8:1 "Hence, now there is no condemnation for those who are in Christ Jesus."

Wow! What did that mean to me? God was not condemning me? God loved me unconditionally? I read further in Romans 8 and it changed my life:

Romans 8:33-35, 37-39 "Who will bring a charge against God's chosen ones? It is God who acquits us. Who will condemn? It is Christ [Jesus] who died, rather, was raised, who also is at the right hand of God, who indeed intercedes for us. What can separate us from the love of Christ? Will anguish, or distress, or persecution, or famine, or nakedness, or peril, or the sword? ... No, in all these things we conquer overwhelmingly through him who loved us. For I am convinced that neither death, nor life, nor angels, nor principalities, nor present things, nor future things, nor powers, nor height, nor depth, nor any other creature will be able to separate us from the love of God in Christ Jesus our Lord."

What did that mean to me? It meant that I could forgive myself for not being perfect because God loved me unconditionally. When that went from my head to my heart, it changed me from having to prove myself to God to just being me. I felt relaxed and not stressed all the time.

My inner healing was enhanced when I read

Ephesians:

> Ephesians 1:3-5 "Blessed be the God and Father of our Lord Jesus Christ, who has blessed us in Christ with every spiritual blessing in the heavens, as he chose us in him, before the foundation of the world, to be holy and without blemish before him. In love he destined us for adoption to himself through Jesus Christ in accord with the favor of his will."

That was almost too much for me to comprehend. I was blessed and holy. I received grace and spiritual blessings because I was His adopted son! How could I be depressed or feel badly about myself if I meditated on this truth? I realized that I had to surrender to the love of my Father in heaven, a Father who I had never connected with or even wanted to connect with or have a relationship.

While this was life-changing, the devil wanted me to continue to live in bondage. There was an inner war going on inside me that continues to this day. This meant that I had to surrender my unconscious to the will of my Father for me to experience inner healing. The importance of 2

Corinthians 10:4-6 became obvious:

> "For the weapons of our battle are not of flesh but are enormously powerful, capable of destroying fortresses. We destroy arguments and every pretension raising itself against the knowledge of God, and take every thought captive in obedience to Christ, and are ready to punish every disobedience, once your obedience is complete."

The enemy always tried to put thoughts into my head that I am not loveable, not worthy, not forgiven or worse. Reading and memorizing these Scriptures is important. We must understand how much God loves us in order to grow in holiness. God will show us His love when we open our hearts to Him and look for it. Every time we think otherwise, that God doesn't love us unconditionally when we sin, know that the enemy is trying to get us discouraged and defeat our mission.

It is important that we build spiritual muscle. One of the critical areas for us is the sacraments. We can't have the forgiveness we need within our minds unless we are healed through the sacraments. This is especially true for the Sacrament of Reconciliation. This is absolutely necessary for us to have inner healing. Without reconciliation, it is impossible to have the inner healing we need to be made whole.

I can't recommend enough the importance of having a spiritual director. We simply need someone to go deep into our hearts and souls and give us feedback that will heal us emotionally and spiritually. I often reflect on St. Paul's words in Romans:

> Romans 7:15-20, "What I do, I do not understand. For I do not do what I want, but I do what I hate. Now if I do what I do not want, I concur that the law is good. So now it is no longer I who do it, but sin that dwells in me. For I know that good does not dwell in me, that is, in my flesh. The willing is ready at hand, but doing the good is not. For I do not do the good I want, but I do the evil I do not want. Now if [I] do what I do not want, it is no longer I who do it, but sin that dwells in me."

We need the ultimate healer, our Lord Jesus

Christ. We try to do what God wants but we fall short of the mark. We need every tool. A spiritual director will help us understand the triggers to sin. He or she will assist in building maturity and spiritual muscle to overcome the temptation to sin. It is important to try to find someone we can see on a regular basis if we want to be used by the Lord effectively and have our ministries grow and flourish. Ask your pastor who they recommend!

I truly believe that the Blessed Mother and the rosary are absolutely critical for our inner healing. We have a spiritual mother who loves us and will intercede for us. Praying the rosary every day will help protect us from evil and give us the grace to do God's will. I can't emphasize enough the importance of having a relationship to Mary. Many devout teachers of our faith, including holy priests, have said the quickest way to become a saint and achieve holiness is through the Blessed Mother. If you don't have a relationship with her, ask her to come into your life. Pray the rosary daily and expect your life to change in a profound way.

One of the most important tools for us in respect

to inner healing is to pray the Scriptures. Truly read it every day and expect it to take over your life. Without reading and imbibing the word of God, I fall prey to my own emotions. What does Scripture do for us?

> Hebrews 4:12 "Indeed, the word of God is living and effective, sharper than any two-edged sword, penetrating even between soul and spirit, joints and marrow, and able to discern reflections and thoughts of the heart."

I believe that if we truly understand the word of God, we would have it with us at all times. More importantly, we would read, memorize and use it on a daily basis. When will speak the words of Scripture we speak the power of the Lord through the Holy Spirit. As Catholics, most of us did not grow up with this mentality. The word of God was simply something to listen to at Mass.

An example of the power of Scripture is the teaching of love. We know that God is love! We learn that in 1 John. With love, we are healed emotionally. We learn from 1 Corinthians the importance of love:

1 Corinthians 13:4-8 "Love is patient, love is kind. It is not jealous, [love] is not pompous, it is not inflated. It is not rude, it does not seek its own interests, it is not quick-tempered, it does not brood over injury, it does not rejoice over wrong-doing but rejoices with the truth. It bears all things, believes all things, hopes all things, and endures all things.

"Love never fails. If there are prophecies, they will be brought to nothing; if tongues they will cease; if knowledge it will be brought to nothing."

Think how our lives would change if we spent our time reading Scripture and having these words in our hearts rather than if we just watched television or spent time on our phones, tablets or computers. This is expressed clearly in Hebrews 5:12-14:

"Although you should be teachers by this time, you need to have someone teach you again the basic elements of the utterances of God. You need milk [and] not solid food. Everyone who lives on milk lacks experience of the word of righteousness, for he is a child. But solid food is for the mature, for those whose faculties are trained by practice to discern good and evil."

The word of God heals us and inspires us to do the will of God. We learn about the power of the tongue in Proverbs 18:21:

"Death and life are in the power of the tongue;

those who choose one shall eat its fruit."

And also James 3:5-11:

"In the same way the tongue is a small member and yet has great pretensions.

"Consider how small a fire can set a huge forest ablaze. The tongue is also a fire. It exists, among our members as a world of malice, defiling the whole body and setting the entire course of our lives on fire, itself set on fire by Gehenna. For every kind of beast and bird, of reptile and sea creature, can be tamed and has been tamed by the human species, but no human being can tame the tongue. It is a restless evil, full of deadly poison. With it we bless the Lord and Father, and with it we curse human beings who are made in the likeness of God. From the same mouth come blessing and cursing. This need not be so, my brothers. Does a spring gush forth from the same opening both pure and brackish water?"

This teaching is critical for inner healing of forgiveness. If we forgive ourselves emotionally and forgive others, we must guard every word we say. Only focus on the positive, what is going to build up our relationships and our image of ourselves.

Jesus wants to heal us, but we must want to be healed emotionally. To forgive is to desire forgiveness. Jesus died on the Cross for us. He did not create "junk" but someone who is blessed, holy and full of love. Ask Jesus to go deep into your heart and mind and heal you emotionally. Go back as far as necessary to sweep out anything that is not of the Lord. He loves us passionately!

CHAPTER 7
HEALING OF MEMORIES

Jesus tells us over and over that we are to live a life of grace, a life of healing and a life of abundance. Jesus wants to heal us emotionally and heal our deepest wounds and memories.

One of the most important areas and biggest obstacles is the healing of our memories. It prevents us from receiving the grace that God wants to give us. It often leads to an attitude of not wanting to forgive because of our deep wounds and pain.

Think about a memory that is particularly difficult to forget and has caused pain and challenges for you emotionally. Don't know what it is? Ask

God to reveal it to you. For me it was my inability to express myself as a small child and having my father and a room full of adults laughing at me.

When you recall your painful memory, put Jesus at the center of it. Picture His face smiling at you. Look at the entire room and what is happening. When the pain gets too severe continue to focus on Jesus. Receive the comfort of His love. Walk over to Him and have Him hug you and reassure you of His love for you. Then ask God to heal you of that memory.

In order to be healed, we need to get whatever help we need to get beyond the pain. Often that can mean professional help. It is critical that we understand that God's miracles flow through psychologists and psychiatrists. Burying our memories is never the right solution. We can't continue to do the same thing and expect to get a different result.

My family and I spent a lot of time in therapy. I am not ashamed of it. In fact, I highly recommend therapy for many if not most people. If you find yourself engaging in addictive behaviors and don't know why and feel you are stuck, seek professional help. Look at it this way:

if you had a medical issue, wouldn't you go to a medical doctor? If you have an issue of dealing with painful memories, you also need professional help.

Healing of memories is a process. It is not going to happen without prayer. Ask the Lord in contemplative prayer to show you what memories are causing negative behaviors in your life. For most of us, these memories are in our unconscious. They are too painful to deal with emotionally so we bury them. The problem? They come up in our behavior without us realizing it. They cause anger and we don't know why or addictive behaviors that we can't seem to control.

Once we have identified the painful memory and the emotions connected to it, it is critical that we go to Mass on a regular basis to get the grace needed to get past the wound. The Eucharist is the single best solution for healing of any kind, especially healing of memories. Why do we not realize that? Most of us wouldn't want to miss eating and drinking, but we think we don't have to receive the Body and Blood of Jesus on a routine basis. Wrong! Without it we are too weak to overcome emotional trauma in our lives.

Mass is not the only critical sacrament. Frequent reconciliation is necessary for God's miracles to flow through us and heal our memories and addictions. We need to look with spiritual eyes on the importance of reconciliation. To make a good reconciliation, it takes a lot of upfront prayer asking God to reveal to you what is blocking you from achieving the healing required. We prepare for reconciliation by opening ourselves up by reflecting on sin and darkness in our lives and asking for the light of Christ. One simple question is: what does God want to give me in respect to forgiveness and healing? Often our answer is "I don't have a clue." That only means we haven't spent enough time in prayer. Some priests recommend an extensive reconciliation that encompasses our entire life. While this might not be the right solution for you, it is helpful in looking at patterns in our lives that are blocking memories that need to be healed by Jesus.

Many of us have deep trauma in our lives from childhood. Often this leads to shame and not feeling good about ourselves. Most of us want to bury these memories and emotions and never deal with them again. Many people feel that if there is anything which makes us feel bad about ourselves it should be avoided at all costs. Our prayer to God should be to overcome our shame and even guilt for our part in whatever happened and ask for it to come to the surface.

It is common that we have deep guilt for what we have done but have not forgiven ourselves. Perhaps we have been unfaithful to a spouse or in a relationship, lied in order to achieve personal gain or cheated in some endeavor. Whatever we did, we feel bad about ourselves and just want to forget it. Now is the time to get past the guilt and pain. Yes, only God can through His intervention cause that to happen. In other words, through His miracles.

In being healed of our painful memories, we must trust in His love. God's love is unconditional and eternal. I am precious in His eyes because He made us in His image and has given us every spiritual blessing. His desire is for us to be holy, in order for us to achieve the purpose of our lives. God wants to break our bondage to our painful memories. He desires us to have complete freedom. He knows what needs to be healed in our lives. Just let God in and see the miracles flow!

In today's world, many of the painful memories involve sexual issues. Pornography use is a rampant sin and a crisis today. Many people don't want to deal with the reasons why they let pornography, sexual immorality or masturbation into their lives. It is a huge problem that has invaded our church and other denominations as well.

Do you live a double life? On the surface you look like a strong Catholic Christian but in reality you are leading a secret life? This secret behavior has led to sinful habitual behavior that you can't control. You tell yourself that this is the last time, but it is not. You fall back into the sinful behavior time and time again. What must change? You must let God heal you of the root cause of the sinful behavior. It is something that happened to us, often from our childhood, that has to be healed.

In order to be healed we need to understand how much God wants to forgive us and heal us. The moment that we feel sorrow for our part of our sinful behavior and desire forgiveness and healing we begin the process of reconciliation with God. We begin to experience the tremendous compassion, love, forgiveness and mercy of God. We are in the process of being transformed into the son or daughter of God healed of emotional wounds.

One of the challenges of the healing of memories is the denial that we have a problem. We also put conditions on what it would take us to forgive, conditions that are usually impossible to achieve. The problem is we often have some level of depression that can paralyze us. We want to get past the memory once it has surfaced, but don't know how it get past it.

We are angry but don't know why. We have anxiety that someone may find out our secrets. This can lead to depression and addictive behaviors. It also leads to physical problems such as high blood pressure, cardiovascular issues and many other physical ailments, including cancer. This is the reason why it is so critical that we not bury our emotional memories but deal with them.

In the process of being healed of memories we have to ask God for the grace for this miracle to happen. However, asking isn't enough. We have to expect that we will receive this miracle.

Mark 11:24 "Therefore, I tell you, all that you ask for in prayer believe that you will receive it and it shall be yours."

God is merciful and wants to heal our memories. There are the A, B, C's of mercy. The A is **asking** for His mercy. God wants us to approach Him in prayer on a constant basis, repenting of our sins, asking for more faith and asking God to pour out His mercy on us.

The B is to **be** merciful. As we are merciful to those who have hurt us emotionally, so we receive mercy. When this mercy flows through us, we can let it flow through others. God wants us to be the personification of His love. To be merciful when we have been wronged leads to tremendous blessings in our lives.

The C is to **completely** trust in Jesus. The graces of His healing of memories and mercy of ourselves and others occur in abundance when we ask Jesus for more trust in Him. The more we trust in Jesus, the more healing we will receive, especially the healing of memories.

We must never forget Matthew 7:7:

"Ask and it will be given to you, seek and

you shall find, knock and the door will be opened to you."

When we ask God to reveal our painful memories, He will do so. When we seek for them to be healed, it will happen. The entire process must be filled with the love of Jesus through the power of the Holy Spirit.

One of the challenges for us is that we ask but don't really expect anything to happen. When we ask we must expect it to happen!

> 1 John 5:14-15 "We have this confidence in him, that if we ask anything according to his will, he hears us. And if we know that he hears us in regard to whatever we ask, we know that what we have asked him for is ours."

It is faith that moves mountains. It is excuses that keep us paralyzed. In the fifth chapter of John we see the story of the crippled man and the pool of Bethesda. He tells Jesus:

> John 5:7 "Sir, I have no one to put me into the pool when the water is stirred up; while I am on my way, someone else gets down there before me."

Jesus saw it as an excuse and not something that couldn't be healed. He replied, "Rise, take up your mat, and walk."

This is also true in respect to the healing of memories. We might think it is impossible and come up with so many reasons why it can't happen, all of which are not true. With Jesus, all things are possible. Jesus is always the solution. He is God. He is, as reflected in John 14:6, "the way and the truth and the life."

When we have our memories healed, we are positively impacted in many ways. We feel better about ourselves, other people and our relationship with God. It does take believing it will happen. It takes God's intercession, or in other words, His grace and miracles.

CHAPTER 8
FORGIVENESS THROUGH
FASTING AND FEASTING

For most Catholics, fasting is a foreign concept. The closest most of us get to it is during Lent. We give up chocolate or something similar and believe we are doing a great job. It can be hard for us to take fasting seriously.

How does fasting relate to forgiveness and miracles? In my experience, I believe that for us to be successful with fasting, it is only through the grace of God and what I would call a miracle. If you are like me, you would call any success with fasting a miracle. However, in order to take our spirituality seriously, it has to happen.

Indeed, the discipline of fasting releases favor

from the Lord and blessings in our life. Our ministries are set on fire when we fast.

> Acts 13: 2-3 "While they were worshiping the Lord and fasting, the holy Spirit said, 'Set apart for me Barnabas and Saul for the work to which I have called them.' Then completing their fasting and prayer, they laid hands on them and sent them off."

What is fasting? While there are many types of fasting, primarily, for our purposes, fasting is giving up food for a spiritual purpose. When we fast, we get closer to God and develop greater intimacy with Him. It is fasting that opens the door to many miracles. It is fasting that gives us strength to endure trials. It is fasting that will lead to the miracle of forgiveness.

Prayer and fasting are important keys to spiritual breakthrough. Much of this is protection against evil spirits who attack us, which includes a spirit of not being able to forgive. We see this in the story of the healing of a boy with a demon.

> Matthew 17: 14-20 "When they came to the crowd a man approached, knelt down before him, and said, 'Lord, have pity on my son, for he is a lunatic and suffers severely; often he falls into fire, and often

into water. I brought him to your disciples, but they could not cure him. Jesus said in reply, 'O faithless and perverse generation, how long will I be with you? How long will I endure you? Bring him here to me.' Jesus rebuked him and the demon came out of him, and from that hour the boy was cured. Then the disciples approached him in private and said, 'Why could we not drive it out?' He said to them, 'Because of your little faith. Amen, I say to you, if you have faith the size of a mustard seed, you will say to this mountain, 'Move from here to there,' and it will move. Nothing will be impossible for you.'"

Ever notice that when you are under attack, you either want to eat more or do something against the commandments? It takes a great of discipline to be holy. We are under assault by the enemy who wants to defeat us. This often happens when someone does something of which we disapprove. Our ability to get angry or not forgive goes up dramatically.

When we look at Scripture, we see different lengths of fasting. Joshua had a 40-day fast, Daniel 21 days, Paul had up to 14 days, Peter three days and, of course, Jesus had a fast for 40 days in the desert. This, some believe, implies an absolute fast, normal fast and the partial fast.

An absolute fast is extreme and should only be done with supreme caution and prayer. We need to be sure that the Lord is calling us to this type of fast. However, when we consider the degree of animosity and lack of forgiveness we have in some relationships, this type of fast may be necessary. Consult your physician if you feel led to have this degree of fast.

The absolute fast is severe and usually means no food or water for a short period of time. Again, medical consultation and supervision is required. In this case, as with all fasts, there should be ongoing and persistent prayer. I would call this the beginning of fervent prayer, which is intense prayer from the heart that leads us into a much closer relationship with God. If there is a demonic spirit attacking us and giving us feelings of hatred or a lack of forgiveness, this type of fast can be effective.

A normal fast is what people can do to improve personal spirituality. This is going without food for a certain period of time or number of days. Drinking water is necessary and many times clear liquids, such as broth or fruit juices, accompany this fast. Again, consult your physician to make sure this is something that fits with your current health status.

A partial fast is what many of us are familiar with because of what we do during Lent. This is giving up particular foods or certain liquids for period of time. It is important that through prayer, we determine what types of food or drink we fast from and what length of time. During our prayer, we need to focus on what area we need to be healed in respect to our challenges with forgiveness.

When we are under attack and experience spiritual warfare, this type of fast is important. We see this in the Book of Daniel when he and his companions did not eat meats and sweets from the king's table but only had vegetables and water. This was for 10 days followed by another fast that included no sweets, meat or wine for three weeks. This entire time Daniel focused on prayer. This led to God's miracles and his prayer being answered by an angel.

Often challenges with forgiveness are generational and rooted deep in our unconscious. We need drastic changes in our prayer and the type of fasting that will lead to miracles. We see this in the Book of Jonah and the story of Nineveh. You may remember that Jonah was not thrilled about going to Nineveh to tell them of their wickedness. All too often the Lord tells us to do something and we say, "No way."

Jonah wanted to go to a city called Tarshish, not exactly in God's plan. It is God's plan that we do what we are led and told to do for His glory. Unfortunately, we are often rebellious, stubborn and sinful. Despite knowing that he was doing the wrong thing, Jonah decided to get on a ship headed to Tarshish. You may remember the story. A storm occurred because Jonah was fleeing from the Lord.

Finally the men on the ship had taken enough of Jonah's disobedience and threw him into the sea where a great fish swallowed Jonah for three days and nights. God was not done with Jonah and once again told him to go to Nineveh.

How many times has the Lord told you to forgive someone and you have refused? Some people I know have held grudges for so many years it doesn't seem possible. Brother against brother, cousin against cousin, daughters against fathers and mothers, sons the same. Friends that drink the poison of not forgiving longtime friends due to behavior that they felt inappropriate.

Have we learned our lesson yet? The story of Jonah was to show us that in spite of our rebellious and sinful behavior we can repent and turn back to the Lord. This can lead to great miracles and dramatic changes in our lives.

Jonah 3: 1-10 "The word of the LORD

came to Jonah a second time: Set out for the great city of Nineveh, and announce to it the message that I will tell you. So Jonah set out for Nineveh, in accord with the word of the LORD. Now Nineveh was an awesomely great city; it took three days to walk through it. Jonah began his journey through the city, and when he had gone only a single day's walk announcing, 'Forty days more and Nineveh shall be overthrown,' the people of Nineveh believed God; they proclaimed a fast and all of them, great and small, put on sackcloth.

"When the news reached the king of Nineveh, he rose from his throne, laid aside his robe, covered himself with sackcloth, and sat in ashes. Then he had this proclaimed throughout Nineveh: 'By decree of the king and his nobles, no man or beast, no cattle or sheep, shall taste anything; they shall not eat, nor shall they drink water. Man and beast alike must be covered with sackcloth and call loudly to God; they all must turn from their evil way and from the violence of their hands. Who knows? God may again repent and turn from his blazing wrath, so that we will not perish.' When God saw by their actions how they turned from their evil way, he repented of the evil he had threatened to do to them; he did not carry it out."

This powerful story is a critical one for us. It teaches that we can run away from the Lord but we can't hide. How long will we hold onto our bitterness? If we do, we will not follow what the Lord is asking us to do. Forgive without reservation. Forgive in the same way that God has forgiven us. When we finally forgive, miracles and blessings will flow into our lives. It is a guarantee. God is a good God who wants to bless us and give us incredible blessings.

One of the major areas polluting our spirits and our lives is sexual sin. This includes the epidemic of pornography. There are many people who have caught their spouses or those close to them in pornography or sexual sin. They feel they can't forgive them. Or perhaps you can't forgive yourself of your inability to get past sexual sin.

In the Book of Judges, it was a time of great sexual sin. In the land of Gibeah, which belonged to the Benjamites, people were engaging in lewd homosexual acts. These men surrounded the house of a Levite to sexually abuse him. They ended up brutally raping and murdering a concubine. All the tribes of Israel rose up to punish the land of Benjamin. At first they were being defeated. God sent the prophet Phinehas with a message to both fast and pray. All the men fasted for 24 hours and broke the power of the sin and defeated their enemies.

There are evil spirits behind sexual sin and pornography. There are evil spirits behind adultery, which is often due to sins of lack of forgiveness. All of these can and will be broken through prayer and fasting. It is critical that strongholds are broken. Prayer is critical but often fasting is also needed to break through sexual additions such as pornography, homosexuality, adultery and fornication.

When we have challenges and feel we don't know what to do, we can look at the Book of Joel, fast and expect miracles.

Joel 1:14 "Proclaim a holy fast!

Call an assembly!

Gather the elders,

all who dwell in the land,

to the house of the LORD, your God,

and cry out to the LORD!"

In 3:1 we learn what God can do when we fast:

"It shall come to pass

I will pour out my spirit upon all flesh.

Your sons and daughters will prophesy,

your old men will dream dreams,

and your young men will see visions."

When we fast, incredible blessings will occur. These blessings will lead to many miracles. Another example of the depth of fasting is when we consider the messages from our Blessed Mother at Medjugorje. She mentions the word fasting more than 100 times. Some of the examples include the power of fasting in "stopping wars, reducing punishments from God, sanctifies us to receive the holy Spirit, keeps Satan from conquering us, brings the kingdom of God among us, for the coming of Jesus, we will be stronger in faith, helps us love God above everything, and purifies our hearts from sins in the past."

While fasting from food is a critical part of our spiritual growth, there are other things we can fast from and feast on to help and strengthen us to be able to forgive. For example, we can fast from judging others and feast on seeing Christ within them. It is important to fast from anger and feast on forgiveness. We often complain about other people but we can feast on appreciating them. Instead of being bitter toward those who offend us, we can be thankful to the gifts they are to us. At times we gossip about people who have hurt us, but we can go out of our way only to say something nice or nothing at all.

For many of us, we have a life of wishing and hoping. We want to change but we don't know what to do. We want to be close to God and do His will but not change our ways. The old saying is "we can't have our cake and eat it, too." For me, this means changing from old ways where we struggle with forgiveness to radically adopting a change in prayer and adding to it a discipline of fasting.

When we add fasting to our pursuit of holiness we add a huge spiritual weapon. Why did Jesus fast before he faced the devil in the desert? Fasting gives us strength against the enemy and guides us. The Holy Spirit comes upon us when we fast. When we fast we act in the way the Lord has taught us. It is this level of holiness that will transform us into people of forgiveness and peace. We truly become warriors for the Lord and live out our Baptism and Confirmation!

CHAPTER 9
HEALING OF THE FAMILY TREE

In recent years, there have been many seminars and talks regarding the necessity of "healing the family tree." How many families do you know of that have a history of grudges, feuds and a general lack of forgiveness? It is so sad to me that the enemy's influence can be so strong that generation after generation continues its animosity towards a group of people. If you ask members of one family why they hold onto the hostility they have toward another family, often they couldn't tell you. It is something that happened so long ago that few remember the origin. If they do remember, then they need to constantly remind each other of the reason why they have the hatred. It is time to break this evil! It is time to break the bondage the devil has on you and/or your family. It is time to break the chains of lack of forgiveness.

Would you agree with me that it would be a "miracle" for this to occur? Most people who are embedded in this history of animosity and hatred don't have a clue how to get out of it. They think it is impossible. Or, if they want to get out of the lack of forgiveness in their lives, they are afraid that their family might find out and see them as traitors.

Good news! With Jesus all things are possible. You are blessed! You have been called to read this book! You are chosen to break the cycle of ill feelings and be a critical part of healing of your family tree. God loves you and your family, but He also loves the people who are the targets of lack of forgiveness.

It is important to memorize this Scripture and remind yourself that you have a mission to be the light of Christ to your family.

> John 15:16 "It was not you who chose me, but I who chose you and appointed you to go bear fruit that will remain, so

that whatever you ask the Father in my name, he may give you."

You are on a mission of forgiveness for Christ! Doesn't that change your attitude on the importance of healing your family?

Do you feel called? Do you understand that "if not you than whom?" It is not enough to wish and hope that healing of your family will happen. You must pray, pray, pray and expect miracles of healing of the lack of forgiveness in your heart. Then when it has happened to you, try to change others in your family, usually one heart at a time.

You are an instrument for your family to be restored to health. It could be your immediate family or extended family. Remember, God wants to restore you and your family with total spiritual and emotional healing.

Jeremiah 30: 18-22 "Thus says the LORD:

See! I will restore the fortunes of Jacob's tents,

on his dwellings I will have compassion;

a city shall be rebuilt upon its own ruins,

a citadel restored where it should be.

From them will come praise,

the sound of people rejoicing.

I will increase them, they will not decrease,

I will glorify them, they will not be insignificant.

His children shall be as of old,

his assembly shall stand firm in my presence,

I will punish all his oppressors.

His leader shall be one of his own,

and his ruler shall emerge from his ranks.

He shall approach me when I summon him:

Why else would he dare

approach me?—oracle of the LORD!

You shall be my people,

and I will be your God."

Believe! It will happen in your family when you surrender to the Lord all that you have in your heart and soul.

Jesus told us in John 10:10 that He has come to give us life and life abundantly. How is this possible if the sins of our ancestors are causing us to be enslaved by sins of our family tree?

> Lamentations 5:7 "Our ancestors, who sinned, are no more;
>
> but now we bear their guilt."

Pope St. John Paul II urged us to face head on the sins of past generations. He reminded us of Leviticus 26:40:

> "They will confess their iniquity and the iniquity of their ancestors in their treachery against me and in their continued hostility toward me."

We need to trust in the love and healing of Jesus. He will answer our prayers to heal our family tree.

> Psalm 79: 8 "Do not remember against us the iniquities of our forefathers;

let your compassion move quickly ahead
of us,

for we have been brought very low."

We are all very adroit of physical laws, such as the
law of gravity. In addition to physical laws, there
are spiritual laws which are equally true. If you
read and pray these verses in Deuteronomy 5: 9-
10, the power of the words ring true.

> "For I, the LORD, your God, am a jealous
> God, bringing punishment for their
> parent's wickedness on the children of
> those who hate me, down to the third
> and fourth generation, but showing love
> down to the thousandth generation of
> those who love me and keep my
> commandments."

It is clear. We need to do our part to love the
Lord with all our heart, soul, mind and strength.
However, what can we do regarding the sins of
our ancestors and how they impact us?

Prayer and belief is the beginning of all healing.
Ask for the Lord to break the bondage of past
sins. Ask Him also to reveal to you what sins are
the ones that need to be overcome. It could be

sexual sin or other sins of the flesh. It could be an alcohol or drug addiction that needs to be broken.

I strongly recommend you diagram at least three generations to get a sense of recurring patterns of sin that need to be healed. In doing this critical prayer process, it is also important to focus on the gifts and blessings of your family. You can strengthen these blessings in your own life. Claim them and expect God to use them in your life and ministry. It could be the gift of wisdom, faith, organization, leadership or many others.

Examine the areas that need to be healed. It is important to be truthful and be led by the Lord in prayer. There is no doubt that God will reveal to you the truth of your family. As you know, Jesus told us that He is the way, the truth and the life, and that His truth will set us free.

What are some of the critical areas that often need to be healed in our families? These areas will definitely be a huge step forward in our personal healing and in giving us the strength to forgive those who have wounded us. The healing of our family tree will transform us and our ministry as we receive God's love and healing!

1. **Occult bondage**. Unfortunately, this is far more common than most of us realize. It is a reality that those in our family tree who perhaps we don't even know existed gave themselves to demonic forces such as fortune tellers, tarot cards, Ouija boards and worse. Once the enemy has entered a family it takes deep prayer and deliverance to set it free.

2. **Addictions**. This is so common for families. The obvious ones are addictions to alcohol, drugs, sex, money, work and even some hobbies. Anything that is an addiction and brings you further away from Jesus needs to be broken in your family tree and your own life.

3. **Aborted children or other deaths of children** such as stillbirths or miscarriages need to be healed and/or broken, especially if you find it is a pattern in your family tree. It is important to name the children who have been aborted or miscarried. They will be and are intercessors for you and your family. It is important that they be part of your life, even if it is painful at first. God will give you the grace and healing to include them as part of your prayer life.

4. **Abandoned family members**. This is a sin and poison in many families. There are family members who were or are mentally ill, hospitalized, in prison, living alone, part of divorces and for many other reasons are isolated from other family members. Ask for forgiveness if you are one of the people who have abandoned them either now or in the past.

5. **Lack of forgiveness**. As we have said, this is a poison in the family tree that needs to be healed through prayer. This is often seen in many generations and needs deep and fervent prayer. Depending on the severity of the forgiveness issue, it may be years in order for it to truly take root, but it WILL happen if we are persistent.

6. **Mental health issues**. One major example of mental health history is suicide. Unfortunately, this is also all too common in families and needs to be broken immediately. Satan tries to inflict his pain and suffering in this area to break the spirit of families. If your family has been afflicted in this way, don't give up. God will heal you and your family if you pray and believe.

7. **Rejection of God**. This is an area that many people ignore. It is a deep sin that needs healing in families. Many people, perhaps someone in your family, have joined religions that are hostile to the truth or simply have lost all faith. Pray for them to find the truth if they are living and forgive them if they are not living. God will bless your existing family with the gift of faith when you are fervent and persistent with your prayer.

There are seven steps for healing of the family tree that will enhance your ability for you and your family to receive the gift of forgiveness.

1. **Surrender to the unconditional love of the Father**. It is so critical that we be an empty vessel that God can use in a powerful way. Think of two glasses, one empty and the other filled with water. Which one can God fill up? God can do anything, but when we fill ourselves up with our own will and desires, it is easy to leave God out of it. Empty yourself and let God fill you with His grace and will. Think of the vine and the branches in John 15.

Jesus tells us we can't do anything without Him.

For me, my surrender truly started at age 28. A co-worker had given his life to Jesus and I realized he had what I didn't have, a total commitment and personal relationship with Jesus. When I surrendered all of me, and meant it, everything changed. I couldn't stop reading the Bible and telling others about it. I received the gifts and fruits of the Holy Spirit in a way I didn't think possible.

My brothers and sisters, it is time. It is time to totally give your heart and soul to Jesus. What do you have to lose? Nothing! What do you have to gain? Everything! Say this prayer: "Father, I surrender all that I have and all that I am, soul, mind, heart, body, finances, family, friends, work, illness, wants, desires, needs, everything. Take over my life and use me in a powerful way through the intercession of the Blessed Mother and the power of the Holy Spirit in Jesus' name. Amen!"

If you prayed this prayer with your heart and truly meant it, your life would never be the same again. You will be filled with the Holy Spirit in a way you never thought possible. You will desire His presence each and every moment of every day.

2. **Identify generational sin in your family**. God will give you the grace to identify and pray for healing for sins in your family's past and present.

3. **Let the power of the Eucharist transform you**. It is amazing how many people want God to do special favors for them, but don't take the time to receive His Body and Blood on a daily or at least frequent basis. Remember the Lord taught us, "give us this day our daily bread." I firmly believe it wasn't a normal loaf of bread He referenced but the Body and Blood of our Lord and Savior Jesus Christ.

4. **Embrace the Sacrament of Reconciliation**. I can't emphasize this enough. Bondage is broken through frequent reconciliation. The devil can't

defeat the sacraments. The more reconciliation, the more protection we receive! How frequent? Pray, discuss with a priest and decide for yourself what is best for you. Remember, Pope Francis goes once a week!

5. **Receive faith with an expecting heart**. When we pray, it is critical that we expect God to act. This is true for everything but it is especially true for these major sins of our family tree. God is our Father who wants to heal us and our families. Do not forget that He wants this even more than we do!

6. **Turn to the Blessed Mother**. I pray that we all realize how important the Blessed Mother is with our healing and growth. She brings us close to her son Jesus through her prayer, intercession and, most importantly, the rosary. She is a tremendous gift from God to help us achieve holiness and be healed. It is critical that we let her into our hearts with her Immaculate Heart!

7. **Use your gifts to bless and serve God**. You have been created to make a difference. Each of us is unique in having special gifts to serve God and build up the kingdom of God. What are your gifts? If you don't know, pray and ask God and those closest to you. They will tell you what they see are your gifts. Between God and your friends and family, you will know what gifts to use for the Lord. Your heart will confirm it.

Do not give up my brothers and sisters! God is good and wants to heal you and your family tree.

CHAPTER 10
HEALING OF FORGIVENESS
THROUGH GOD'S MERCY

I am convinced that the power of mercy is one of the most important realities of our spiritual lives. Mercy and forgiveness are two sides of the same coin, with love at the center. What is the definition of mercy? "It is the loving kindness, compassion or forbearance shown to one who offends."

The word mercy appears 149 times in Scripture. One of the most powerful uses is in the Beatitudes.

> Matthew 5:7 "Blessed are the merciful, for they will be shown mercy."

This is similar to the words in the Lord's Prayer: "Forgive us our trespasses as we forgive those who trespass against us." To the extent that we let mercy into our lives is the extent that God's merciful grace will flow into us.

Mercy is at the core of forgiveness. To the extent we forgive is the extent we receive God's mercy. We see God's mercy in everything that He does for us. The Father is our role model.

> Luke 6:36 "Be merciful just as [also] your Father is merciful."

In the Old Testament, we see:

> Exodus 34:6 "God [is] gracious and merciful, slow to anger and abounding in love and fidelity."

The inability to forgive is for many people like a chain around them. It is choking their spiritual life and not allowing them to have the life that God wants for them. There are seven critical steps for people to let mercy and forgiveness into their lives.

The first is to open your heart to receive the love of the Father. For many people this step is extremely difficult. They have little experience in being loved by their own fathers or even any male in their lives. What must they do to open their hearts to their heavenly Father? The most important step is to empty their hearts to receive the love of the Father. That sounds easy, but it not. It takes a "miracle," which is God's supernatural intervention in our hearts. However, it necessitates a decision on our part. Do we truly want to be healed? Do we truly want our hearts to be consumed by the love of the Father? If we answer "yes," then we are transformed into the image of Christ. Only then can we truly begin to love ourselves and His people. Only then can we truly love God in the way that we need to be healed. Do not be afraid! God will intervene so that His grace will flow into us!

We are told in Romans 8 that we can call our Father "Abba," which means "daddy." We are also told that nothing will separate us from the love of God! No amount of sin, or rebellion, or rejecting God will matter. Our Father loves us passionately, completely, without compromise or reservation. Our Father is 100% pure love. He is the God of mercy, forgiveness, hope and encouragement.

It is important to learn how to pray differently. We need to meditate on how much God loves us and have that love transform us so that we can truly forgive others and ourselves. We are not perfect. While we are to strive for holiness, it is a process. Forgive yourself. The greatest gift you can give yourself is opening your heart to God's love, forgiveness and mercy. When we love God we are in His presence.

> John 14:23 "Whoever loves me will keep my word and my Father will love him, and we will come to him and make our dwelling with him."

By being one with God, we receive His mercy and are healed of our lack of forgiveness.

The second key for obtaining mercy and forgiveness is to spread the Good News of Jesus Christ! Do you know what is the Good News? I remember someone when asked that question answered with, "If things work out I might barely make Purgatory." No! The Good News is that Jesus died and rose again, took upon Himself the sins of the world, our sins, so that we may have eternal salvation. This is how much He loves us! The ultimate mercy is our salvation when we don't deserve it! Despite our turning our backs on God, He forgives us of our sins. It is a free gift that we must accept.

John 3:16 "For God so loved the world that he gave his only Son so that everyone who believes in him might not perish but have eternal life."

God's mercy and forgiveness must be shouted from the rooftops! God's mercy and forgiveness must be communicated to the world. How many people understand this Scripture?

1 Timothy 2:4 "[God] wills everyone to be saved and to come to the knowledge of the truth."

So many people live in darkness. They are not aware of God's mercy, forgiveness and how He never condemns us but wants us to come to Him.

Romans 8:1 "Hence, now there is no condemnation for those who are in Christ Jesus."

To be an evangelist is not an option for anyone who is serious about their faith in our Lord Jesus Christ. We must want to be holy and to be used to build the kingdom of God. In the Second Vatican Council we are told that "evangelization is at the very heart of the church." Pope St. John Paul II said, "I sense that the moment has come to commit all the church's energies to a new evangelization."

What is the new evangelization? It is to proclaim the Gospel to those closest to us. We are to live the great commission found in Matthew 28:19-20:

> "Go, therefore, and make disciples of all nations, baptizing them in the name of the Father, and of the Son, and of the holy Spirit, teaching them to observe all that I have commanded you. And behold, I am with you always, until the end of the age."

The Gospels are clear. To proclaim the Gospel is the greatest gift of mercy we can give to anyone we encounter. Jesus was very direct:

> Mark 16: 15-18, "He said to them, 'Go into the whole world and proclaim the gospel to every creature. Whoever believes and is baptized will be saved; whoever does not believe will be condemned. These signs will accompany those who believe; in my name they will drive out demons, they will speak new languages. They will pick up serpents [with their hands}, and if they drink any deadly thing, it will not harm them. They

will lay hands on the sick and they will recover.""

I sometimes have poignant dreams. One night, I had a dream in which Jesus was in a beautiful green meadow. He was alone and gestured to have me come to Him. When I did, He embraced me and told me "well done my good and faithful servant."

I did not want to leave His embrace. It was so loving and I felt at peace. He then pointed at a small hill on the horizon. As I was gazing at the hill, suddenly there were people going over the hill and into my sight. At first a few, perhaps five or 10, and then they kept coming. Fifty, a hundred, many hundreds and seemingly a countless number of people coming up and saying to me, "Thank you for telling me about Jesus." I looked at them and said, "I don't know who you are. When did I tell you about Jesus?" They answered that when I spoke at various churches and places they were either there or someone who was there told someone who told them about Jesus. My brothers and sisters, sharing the Good News is a ripple effect. It isn't just the people you speak with, it is the people who find out as the result of many people proclaiming the Gospel and the Good News filtering to them.

Then something happened that shook me up. There was a smaller group of people who approached me, eyes down, who said to me, "You knew the truth but decided not to tell us about Jesus." Wow! It hit me right at the core of my being. I remembered Paul's comments in Acts 20:26-27:

> "And so I solemnly declare to you this day that I am not responsible for the blood of any of you, for I did not shrink from proclaiming to you the entire plan of God."

I realize now, more than ever, that the most merciful thing I can do is to tell people about Jesus, His love and His plan for their salvation!

The third area of mercy which leads to a spirit of forgiveness is to surrender and invite the Holy Spirit into your life. One of my favorite memories occurred a few years ago when my wife and I prayed over about 150 children, ages 6-15, for the "Baptism of the Holy Spirit." One girl in particular was truly changed by the Holy Spirit. We had prayed over the children on a Saturday and a Sunday morning. Afterwards, I was walking through the arena at the Anaheim Convention Center to go to my next talk. I saw this girl, age 7, and her mother running up to me. The mother said, "Deacon, did you pray over my daughter yesterday?" I told her I had. She said her daughter was so excited she could barely sleep. The little girl then looked up at me and asked, "Did you receive the Holy Spirit at Baptism?" I said, "Yes!" She then asked me one of the most interesting questions I have ever heard in ministry: "Deacon, if I received the Holy Spirit at Baptism, then why is He hiding?"

Wow! So important! This girl got to the heart of the issue. The Holy Spirit is able to change our lives, to give us power and transform us.

I answered her, "We have to want the Holy Spirit to be released in us." We receive the Holy Spirit at Baptism and Confirmation, but we must ask the Holy Spirit to be released in our lives. We must want it! When that happens, everything changes. We see in Luke 11 that the Father will give us the Holy Spirit as a gift when we ask for it. It is a tremendous act of mercy that leads to a spirit of forgiveness when we pray for the release of the Holy Spirit and teach others to do the same.

Remember that the Holy Spirit is similar to an action verb. He will teach us what to do and bring us closer to Jesus.

> John 14:26 "The Advocate, the holy Spirit that the Father will send in my name – he will teach you everything and remind you of all that [I] told you."

The fourth area for mercy is living the Corporal Works of Mercy.

> Matthew 25: 35-36, 40 "For I was hungry and you gave me food, I was thirsty and you gave me drink, a stranger and you welcomed me, naked and you clothed me, ill and you cared for me, in prison and you visited me. Amen, I say to you, whatever you did for one of these least brothers of mine, you did for me."

The Holy Spirit will direct and guide you on what to do with the Corporal Works of Mercy. For each person it will be unique and different. I greatly enjoyed the seven years I spent ministering in jails and the time I have spent in Asia visiting and praying for those in prison.

One of the most rewarding things I have ever done is in the area of employment. We created an "employment ministry" at our parish, teaching people how to network, write resumes, interview, use LinkedIn and many other things. So many people didn't know what to do when they lost their jobs. In the last 10-plus years there have been hundreds of people we have helped find work.

Don't be concerned about what to do regarding the Corporal Works of Mercy. Pray and the Holy Spirit will guide you. There are so many things to do and so few people who want to make a difference. Thank you for your "yes!"

The fifth area of mercy to help with your journey of forgiving others and yourself is the Spiritual Works of Mercy. One of them is "pray for the living and the dead." Intercede for those people who you are trying to forgive. The most important thing you can do is to love them by praying for them. What about those who have passed on? Ask for the grace to pray for them. Pray for the souls in Purgatory.

Be an instrument of hope to everyone you encounter. Teach people Romans 8:28:

> "We know that all things work for good for those who love God, who are called according to his purpose."

God will make all things good when we love and trust Him. Give people hope by teaching them to be thankful no matter what is happening in their lives.

> 1 Thessalonians 5:16-18 "Rejoice always. Pray without ceasing. In all circumstances give thanks, for this is the will of God for you in Christ Jesus."

The sixth area for mercy that will soften hearts for Jesus and forgiveness is to give your heart to the Immaculate Heart of Mary. Whatever is happening in your life, by turning to your Spiritual Mother and asking her to intercede for you, will always lead you to peace and a closer relationship with Jesus. She is the Mother of Mercy. The Blessed Mother was clear to St. Bridget of Sweden when she told her, "I am the Queen of heaven and the Mother of mercy."

The seventh area of mercy to strengthen and help us to forgive is the Divine Mercy Chaplet and Novena. We are told to be holy and to be set apart. The Divine Mercy devotion will help you do that and grow in your love of Jesus. It encourages us to consecrate our lives to Jesus and His mercy, holiness and forgiveness. We become instruments of His mercy and forgiveness.

What an act of love from Jesus to us and a great act of love, forgiveness and mercy when we become "Divine Mercy evangelists." Tell people about the special grace available that Our Lord revealed to Saint Faustina regarding Divine Mercy Sunday, which is the Sunday after Easter.

When we receive Holy Communion on Divine Mercy Sunday, go to confession within 20 days of Divine Mercy Sunday, pray for the pope's intentions and have a public devotion to Divine Mercy on Mercy Sunday, we have the equivalent of a complete renewal of baptismal grace in the soul which is complete forgiveness of sins and punishment. This makes our soul "whiter than snow."

Take the time to read the Diary of Saint Faustina. We find the words of Jesus to her saying, "It pleases Me to grant everything they ask of me by saying the Chaplet." Jesus tells her over and over that even the most hardened sinners will receive mercy when they say the Chaplet. Saying the Chaplet at the hour of death will bring great mercy and grace to the person dying "for the sake of the sorrowful passion of my Son."

It is extremely difficult to be merciful and to forgive those who have hurt us. We need spiritual tools like the rosary and the Chaplet of Divine Mercy. Don't be discouraged or give up. God will give you the strength. Expect and experience

God's grace and miracles by forgiving yourself and others!

CHAPTER 11
SPREADING GOD'S
FORGIVENESS AND MERCY

I am convinced that the greatest act of mercy we can give anyone is telling them about God's love, forgiveness and mercy. We were given a commission to spread the Good News of Jesus Christ, that believing in Him and trusting in His resurrection will give us eternal salvation.

When I was five years of age, I remember looking up at the sky and seeing rays of the sun going through the clouds and feeling overwhelming intense love and the presence of Love. I felt that I had been with my Father in heaven and He had sent me on a special mission. I still think it is hard to fathom. God was sending me on a mission of love, forgiveness and mercy.

A couple of years ago, God gave me a series of three dreams. In each of the dreams the Father told me that the most important thing I and our ministry, Spirit Filled Hearts, could do is spread the message of Divine Mercy. In so doing, there would be countless number of souls saved, entering into the kingdom of God.

There have been a number of Scriptures that remind me of my mission. The first is John 15:16-17:

> "It was not you who chose me, but I who chose you and appointed you to go and bear fruit that will remain, so whatever you ask of my Father in my name he may give you. This I command you, love one another."

We are all chosen to bear fruit, to spread the message of love and mercy to the ends of the earth.

We are to love passionately with the love of Jesus. St. Teresa of Calcutta, whom we also know as Mother Teresa, told us in her books and speeches to "love until it hurts." Peter tells us:

> 1 Peter 1:22 "Love one another intensely from a [pure] heart."

He then told us:

> 1 Peter 4:8 "Above all, let your love for one another be intense, because love covers a multitude of sins."

Love changes everything. We can move mountains of sin, lack of forgiveness and animosity through the grace and unconditional love of Jesus.

From the time of our Baptism, we were anointed to make a difference. We received the oil of sacred chrism and anointed to be priest, prophet and king. We were commissioned to sacrifice, as a priest does, our own needs for the good of others. As a prophet, we are to spread the word of God and His Good News. As a king, we are part of the kingdom of God "on earth as it is in heaven."

At confirmation we were "sealed by the Holy Spirit," as we, once again, receive the sacred chrism. The sacrament of confirmation gives us the ability to be "warriors" of Christ. We are battling a ruthless enemy who wants to destroy us. However, we have the tools to defeat the powers of evil. One of the greatest tools? Forgiveness! To forgive those who have harmed us, both emotionally or even physically.

We need to make a decision for Christ and be an agent of mercy and forgiveness. We have not been left orphans!

> John 14:18 "I will not leave you orphans;
> I will come to you."

We have been given the power of the Holy Spirit to be this agent of mercy and forgiveness.

> 1 Corinthians 4:20 "The kingdom of God
> is not a matter of talk but of power."

How do we get this power? By asking for the Holy Spirit and saying "yes" for Him to take over our lives, we release the power of God within us.

> Acts 1:8 "But you will receive power
> when the holy Spirit comes upon you and
> you will be my witnesses … to the ends
> of the earth."

Great miracles of love, mercy and forgiveness will

come when we accept the presence and power of the Holy Spirit within us.

Today, we see struggles in many places in the world. Catholics make up 16% of the world's population with 1.2 billion members. Over the past 100 years, there have been areas of growth but also significant areas of weakness and decline. One such area is Europe, where our Church population has declined. In the United States, we have declined from 84 million to 70 million in the last 18 years.

There is growth in Africa, where there are many miracles, along with renewal and dynamic faith, leading to many vocations. In the last 100 years in Africa the Church has grown from 1% of the population to 21%. In the Congo, there are 31 million Catholics, nearly 50% of the population. Brazil and the Philippines continue to be strong but are under siege by many other denominations and religions.

What is our mission? To spread the message of forgiveness and mercy. We are called to make a difference. It is why we are born! We are to know, love and serve God. I know some of you are thinking, "That's not for me." I'm not qualified, don't know what to say, don't want to offend anyone and others would be better. All of us feel the same at one point. Let someone else do it.

We have to be careful about sins of omission. When God calls us to make a difference it is critical we say "yes" to Him. I believe that in the Book of Revelation when God "wipes every tear from our eyes" it is primarily the sins of omission that are wiped away. After all, Jesus died for our sins.

How can we spread the mercy of Christ? There are seven important steps:

1.   **Our relationship with Jesus**. We need to surrender to His love and let Him take over our lives.   Seek holiness.   Go to Mass and reconciliation as often as you can. Daily pray the rosary and Divine Mercy Chaplet, and read Scripture.

2.   **Have the desire to spread the Gospel of forgiveness and mercy**. Ask God to give you the grace to spread His love, mercy and forgiveness. I believe strongly that the extent you want to be used you will be used.

3. **Pray to become an ambassador of God's love**.

> Mark 12:30-31 "You shall love the Lord your God with all your heart, with all your soul, with all your mind, and with all your strength.
>
> "The second is this: 'You shall love your neighbor as yourself. There is no other commandment greater than these."

Be a pencil for Jesus to flow through you. Pray that your relationships be all of Christ and none of your flesh. Pray love into everyone you encounter. I once learned that a friend of mine had not spoken to his brother in 20 years. I told him how much God loved them both, and that with God's grace, there would be forgiveness and reconciliation. Sure enough, he called his brother and after 20 years they forgave each other, and together loved each other with the love of Jesus. It was a true miracle!

4. **We are called to be obedient**! When God calls us we need to answer Him and do whatever we are commanded to do. In my case, I was called to forgive my father for hurting me emotionally and physically. I was also called to forgive the

people who had me terminated from my job. Both were difficult, but it was God's grace and His work of miracles that had me forgive those who hurt me the most. I was obedient and healed of my lack of forgiveness!

5.   **The power of the Holy Spirit in your life**. Don't water down the Gospel or the power of the Holy Spirit.   Call upon Him to heal your relationships. There is no one above God's love. There is no one who can't be healed or changed.

6.   **Bloom where you are planted and have God work forgiveness whomever you are**. Sometimes spreading God's love, mercy and forgiveness occurs when you least expect it. When I was in formation to become a deacon, I worked as a volunteer chaplain at a local Catholic hospital. I would receive a list of rooms to visit for prayer. It often was more than I had time to visit. The hospital, upon admission, would ask patients if they wanted to declare their religion. Many were Catholic and those would be the ones I would visit.

One day I was walking down the hallway of a hospital ward and I was reading the declared religion of the patients. The ward was a trauma unit. I was walking past a room where the patient was Muslim. I picked up my pace but suddenly the Lord came upon me and said, "Go back to the room of the Muslim and pray with her." I said, "You sure? There are many rooms with Catholics I could visit." Wrong question.

I went into the room and there was a woman who was all alone in the center of the room on a bed. There was a man sitting in a chair against the window. It was her brother. He brought me the chair and said, "You're going to need this."

I wasn't sure what to do or say, so I said, "Can I pray with you?" The woman immediately started crying. She told me the story of what had happened. She said that her husband had flown into Los Angeles International Airport the night before. It was late and she asked him if he wanted her to drive. She was with her two daughters and her mother. Her husband said he was fine and wanted to drive. Unfortunately, her husband fell asleep at the wheel along with everyone else in the car. There was a major accident and her husband was killed and the four of them were all seriously injured. She started screaming and said, "I killed my husband! I can never forgive myself!"

Forgiveness, love and mercy are given to everyone regardless of religion or faith. I told her how much God loved her. She ripped a Sacred Heart prayer card out of my hand. She put it to her chest. I started praying that she forgive herself and that she receive the peace of Jesus.

A week later I was back and saw her being pushed in a wheelchair down the hall. She looked at me and called me over. She was smiling from ear to ear. She said that the night after I had prayed with her, she had a dream and saw her husband dressed in white. He told her that he was fine and that everything would be fine with her and to forgive herself. Praise God! It was another incredible miracle of love and forgiveness.

7. **Be a person of invitation**. When someone is hurting and needs love and forgiveness, invite that person to church or to a group of which you might be part. Offer an invitation to coffee or breakfast after Mass. We are called to be people of invitation.

All of us have gifts. We are called to use those gifts. The Parable of the Talents in Matthew 25 is a good example of how we are to use what gifts and talents God has given us and not bury them. We are called to let people know about Jesus.

> Romans 10:14-17 "How can they believe in him of whom they have not heard? And how can they hear without someone to preach? And how can people preach unless they are sent? As it is written, 'How beautiful are the feet of those who bring [the] good news … Faith comes from what is heard, and what is heard comes through the word of Christ.'"

Let us pray to become like the Father of the Prodigal Son, always watching for the moment when we can love unconditionally and forgive without compromise. May we be the witnesses of God's love and mercy throughout our lives.

CHAPTER 12
PRAYER AND FORGIVENESS

One of the most important Scripture passages is one that we dismiss quickly as being seemingly impossible:

1 Thessalonians 5:17 "Pray without ceasing."

How do we live this Scripture and have it be part of our lives? Reflect also on this passage:

John 15:1-5, 7 "I am the true vine, and my Father is the vine grower. He takes away every branch in me that does not bear fruit, and everyone that does he prunes so that it bears more fruit. You

143

are already pruned because of the word that I spoke to you. Remain in me, as I remain in you. Just as a branch cannot bear fruit on its own unless it remains on the vine, so neither can you unless you remain in me. I am the vine, you are the branches. Whoever remains in me and I in him will bear much fruit, because without me you can do nothing. If you remain in me and my words remain in you, ask for whatever you want and it will be done for you."

What does this mean for you? It means that we must be in the presence of God at all times. When we are connected to God (the vine) we are indeed a branch that can "pray without ceasing." This also means that we can forgive with the grace of God because we have God in our hearts. We "remain in him as he remains in us."

What is the best way of remaining in God and having Him in us? The power of praise. So few people truly understand that praise changes everything. What is praise? It is meditating and worshiping the attributes of God. When we praise, we describe who God is, not what He has done for us, which is being thankful.

We were created to praise.

> Isaiah 43:21 "The people whom I formed for myself,
>
> that they might recount my praise."

Everything in us was created for praise.

> Psalm 150:6 "Let everything that has breath
>
> give praise to the LORD!"

All of creation was created to praise God.

> Romans 8:22 "All creation is groaning in labor pains even until now."

We may remember in Scripture when the Pharisees told Jesus to have His disciples stop praising God. He answered:

> Luke 19:40 "I tell you, if they keep silent, the stones will cry out!"

Everything we do, think or act should have praise at the foundation. Praise is to be on our lips constantly.

Hebrews 13: 15 "Through him [then] let us continually offer God a sacrifice of praise, that is, the fruit of lips that confess his name."

We praise God by describing who He is to us. He is the King of Kings, the Lord of Lords, the great I Am, the Alpha and the Omega, the Prince of Peace, the God of Love, our Savior, our Redeemer, our Deliverer, our Healer, our Father, our Rock, our Creator, the Word made Flesh and infinitely more!

When we learn to praise God everything changes in our lives. We no longer are alone but we are filled with the Holy Spirit. When we praise, our lives will never be the same because our attitude is one with the Lord. I believe that it is impossible to be anxious, depressed, discouraged or experience any negative emotion when we are praising the Lord. We are transformed into His image. We truly receive His peace when we praise Him. We grow in our love for Jesus until our lives becomes reflections of His grace and mercy. When we have hatred, animosity, lack of forgiveness and any other negative feeling toward ourselves or other people, it melts away when we learn how to praise!

What do we need to do to have praise be intimately part of our beings? To get the grace to let praise transform us into His image? Let's look at the word "praise" as a way of helping us keep this form of prayer at the core of our thoughts and actions.

The "p" in praise stands for presence. When Adam and Eve sinned, they left the presence of God. They hid and clothed themselves and had to leave the Garden of Eden. We have been trying to get back into the presence of God ever since. In order to get into His presence, we must invite Jesus into our lives on an ongoing basis. We can learn how to praise Him throughout the day and even when we sleep. It is His will that we are connected to Him, and "remain in him as he remains in us."

When we wake up, we can immediately praise Him for the day and the miracles that are coming. We can thank Him for the gift of waking and for our health, our home, our family, our job and everything else in our lives. Let God know how much you love Him.

When we have breakfast, thank Him for the food He has provided you, for having the ability to eat and drink and for having the resources so that you are not starving.

Do whatever you can to attend daily Mass. Praise God for the tremendous gift of His Body and Blood. The entire Mass is one of praise and thanksgiving. While praying at Mass, think of who God is and praise Him for His attributes.

When you drive to work or school, listen to praise music! At stop signs, praise Him for the beauty of what you see and for everything that comes into your mind. Recite the "Litany of Praises."

Visit the Lord in adoration as often as you can. Praise Him during the silence and during your prayers. When you pray the rosary or Divine Mercy Chaplet, use praise as a foundation. Let any lack of forgiveness be healed by praising God for the person in your life who is troubling to you.

During work, praise Him during meetings and phone conversations. Whatever happens, good or bad, praise Him for being your provider, protector and giving you the gift of your job. Praise Him constantly during the day and your blessings will flow beyond anything you can imagine. If there are people at work who you have not forgiven, praise God for bringing them in your life! Yes, this definitely includes your boss and co-workers!

In the evening, instead of watching television, read the Book of Psalms and books or articles that praise God. Pray with your spouse and family and let praise be constantly on your lips and in your heart. Sit alone before the Lord in the Blessed Sacrament and do a Holy Hour.

When you sleep, train yourself to be praising God. When you have dreams that are not of the Lord, you can begin praising God and the dreams will no longer bother you. Begin by saying the name of Jesus over and over. You can add, "I love you, Jesus" and "I trust in you, Jesus," and you will see how your sleep changes to being one with the Lord!

The "r" in praise stands for restoration.

When we praise God, we are well on the way to being restored spiritually, emotionally, mentally and physically. One of the most important aspects of being transformed by praise is forgiving those who have hurt us. This often starts with forgiving ourselves, which can be the most difficult. This will always include those closest to us, including our spouses, children, grandchildren, friends, bosses, co-workers, neighbors, those in our parish and anyone else who God has put in our path.

Whoever God has put in your life, forgive them! What is the best way to forgive? Praise God for them! Praise God that they are in your life and that they are exactly the way they are. Why? Because God is in them and He turns everything into good.

> Romans 8:28 "We know all things work
> for good for those who love God, who
> are called according to his purpose."

Yes, that includes your spouse and children. Instead of trying to change them, praise God for their being the way they are. Love them unconditionally. I have seen this change relationships when marriages are falling apart and children are not speaking to their parents. When we praise God, we forgive, and we restore relationships.

My daughter has always had a strong will. From the time she was born she tried hard to get her way. I remember her being in the backseat of our car at about age three and turning around to the cars behind us and putting up her hand and saying, "Don't follow me!"

Our family, like most families, had major conflicts and trials. My daughter objected to decisions that were being made and decided not to talk to my wife and sometimes me. This went on for seven years. During this time, I thought of families that seemingly got along, daughters who were obedient to their parents. I kept praying that my daughter be transformed into a daughter who did what I wanted her to do. In other words, I wanted to change her into my image of what a daughter was supposed to be.

Wrong! God came to me and told me how sinful I was in desiring this. The Lord told me specifically, "She is the perfect daughter for you and you are the perfect father for her." God had given me a daughter I needed and her the parents she needed to do God's will. God then told me to praise Him for my daughter being exactly the way she was. When I started doing that everything changed! My conservations with her changed dramatically. I was much more loving. While it took time, eventually our relationship changed and she welcomed us into her life. Today, we have a great relationship! Miracles of forgiveness will occur when we praise Him!

Another example of forgiveness through praise involves the pastor of my parish. Prior to him, we had a pastor who everyone, including me, felt was an extremely loving man. Unfortunately, he died at the very young age of 50.

Our community prayed and prayed to get a pastor similar to the one we had. What happened? We got a completely different man with a different personality. It was hard for many people, including me, to know how to treat him. Most people ignored him.

God came to me very powerfully. He said, "Who are you to judge my shepherd, the man I put as the head of your parish? I want you to love him!" I changed my attitude immediately. I began supporting him and giving him attention. What happened? Within two months, I was asked to apply to be a deacon. Because of forgiveness, God blessed me by giving me the grace of Holy Orders and making me a deacon! I have had a great relationship with the pastor for 12 years because I know that he is the shepherd and I am not. Praise God! Now and forever!

The "a" in praise stands for attitude. When we praise God we have an attitude of being grateful. By praising God we have the attitude of seeing the glass half full. When we see the glass half empty, are complaining and trying to change everything, we are never filled with peace and the Holy Spirit in the way that God wants for us. When we praise God we always have the attitude that will bless us and have us grow spiritually. The Psalms tell us over and over that we are born to praise God. We are told in 1 Thessalonians 5: 17-18:

> "In all circumstances give thanks, for this is the will of God for you in Christ Jesus."

When we have the right attitude, we are praising God for everything that is happening to us because we know God is at the center of it. We are enthroned in praise!

The "i" in praise stands for intercession. When we intercede for others we are "standing in the gap." We are entering His gates and presence with praise.

Psalm 100: 4 "Enter his gates with thanksgiving,

his courts with praise.

Give thanks to him, bless his name."

Do you want miracle after miracle to happen in your life? Change your attitude to praising Him at all times instead of petition after petition.

An example of this occurred when I was in Glendale, California at the home in which I grew up. There was a major fire in the hills where the house was located. There were already a number of homes that had burnt down. The firefighters told me that they couldn't save my parents' home.

It was 7 p.m., and I began praising God as the God of fire and wind. I left and went to safety with my father. The next morning I came back and there was no fire and no additional homes had been destroyed. I asked a firefighter what had happened. He told me it was a miracle. No one expected the wind to shift, but at 7 p.m., when I was praying, the wind shifted and the fire burnt itself out. Praise God!

Praise changes everything, which includes

relationships. I have seen many miracles when I praise God. Another one happened when I was in Mexico with Corazon, an organization that builds homes for the poor. We had run out of paint, but had the whole interior left to paint. My fellow volunteers came to me and asked what to do. The only paint they had left was the goo on the side and bottom of one paint bucket. I was startled but started praying and praising God fervently. I told them to add water. They did, applied our new "paint," and to my great surprise the paint color was the same as the paint outside! After half of the room was painted, they came to me with an empty paint bucket and again asked what to do. You guessed it! I said, "Fill it with water!" I was praising God with all my heart and soul! Sure enough, the whole interior was painted with a thick coat of paint! I have many witnesses! Praise God! Now and forever!

The "s" in praise stands for strength. When you feel like giving up because of your pain, lack of forgiveness and struggling relationships, turn to God in praise. In Nehemiah 8:10, we see:

"Rejoicing in the LORD is your strength."

How do we get joy? When we begin praising God

and our life changes! The Psalms show us constantly that the Lord is our strength and our shield. God gives us the strength to endure suffering, trials, death, health problems, difficult relationships and an attitude of lack of forgiveness.

When we praise God, miracles happen. After marching around Jericho seven times, the Israelites began praising God and the city's massive walls fell down. In 2 Chronicles 20, King Jehosaphat prepared his army by appointing singers to praise the holiness of God. In battle they were to praise God, for His mercy endures forever. They won a great victory!

The "e" in praise stands for miracles. When we praise God, we enter into His courts and presence. We do His will by acknowledging who He is and what He is doing for us. I believe that God wants us to live a life of forgiveness and miracles.

I had a boss who was driving me crazy. When I started praising God for my boss, we became best friends and my productivity went through the roof. By forgiving and praising God, I received a major promotion. To me, it was a miracle beyond belief.

Reflect on the biggest challenge of forgiveness you have in your life. Begin praising God for that person and relationship. Do not try to change the person but accept him or her for who they are and what they are doing in your life. Feel the peace and love of the Lord fill your heart and soul. Do that daily for seven days. You will find miracles begin to happen!

CHAPTER 13
THE BATTLEFIELD OF THE MIND

I have an important question to ask you: who wants you to hold onto your feelings of animosity and your unwillingness to forgive? You know it is not the Lord! The enemy wants to hold you in bondage.

Whether you realize it or not, you are in a battle with the enemy of God, Satan and the demons associated with him. Saint Peter informs us what we are up against:

> 1 Peter 5:8 "Be sober and vigilant. Your opponent the devil is prowling around

like a roaring lion looking for [someone] to devour."

The devil doesn't want us to trust or rely on Jesus. He wants us to live in fear, defeat our purpose in our lives and negate our ministries. If the devil can't get our souls, then he wants us to not assist others in finding Christ. One of the major tactics of the enemy is for us to live a life where we don't forgive: ourselves, God and other people. It takes a miracle for us to truly forgive. It takes the grace of Jesus to forgive and to defend us in battle.

Lack of forgiveness is a poison that is often sent with hatred from the devil. Good news! Jesus has defeated the devil! He wants us to live a life of abundance.

John 10:10 "I came so that they might have life and have it more abundantly."

Jesus wants us to have the strength and power to defeat the attacks against us.

Philippians 4:13 "I have the strength for everything through him who empowers me."

Philippians 4:19 tells us how much we are given the resources to live life with joy:

> "My God will fully supply whatever you need, in accord with his glorious riches in Christ Jesus."

Each day we have decisions to make: do we move toward God, which is called "consolation," or away from God, which is called "desolation?" Psychologists tell us that each day we have 2,000 or more choices to make. Many of those choices involve forgiveness. Instead of being sarcastic or answering with bitterness, we choose silence and forgiveness.

Satan is the father of lies. One of the biggest lies is that we are not forgiven. If Satan wants to remind us of our past, then we should remind him of his future! Do not fear but embrace the truth! You are loved unconditionally and forgiven of your sins, which are wiped clean and forgotten! Should we not do the same with others and ourselves?

The enemy wants to control our minds. Ever notice that when we find ourselves wanting to forgive others or ourselves that we have a whisper in our ear as to why we shouldn't forgive? The enemy often tells us that we need to be treated differently. It could be that we aren't "respected." How about, "I shouldn't be talked to that way?" Ever hear that one whispered to you or have that thought come into your mind? When that occurs we know that the enemy is at work, trying to control our thoughts and minds.

In order to counter these tactics, we must use the weapons that God has given us to win this battle with the enemy. There are seven steps that lead us to victory on the battlefield of the mind.

The first, and most important, is to **surrender our lives, our hearts and our souls to Jesus**. When I pray over people, the Lord has given me insights through the "word of knowledge," as to whether or not their hearts are open to the Lord's love and healing. Many times there is lack of forgiveness, sin that is serious and unconfessed and weak faith. The first thing I do in these circumstances is ask them to pray the "sinner's prayer" with their hearts and give their life to Jesus. The Lord can't fill what is already filled with people's own desires. We must surrender our hopes, fears, dreams, will, sins, family, finances and anything else we are putting ahead of the Lord. When we are an empty vessel, everything changes. Lack of forgiveness melts away and miracles flow into our lives. If we are not empty of our own flesh, we will not achieve victory on the battlefield of the mind.

> James 1: 7-8 "That person must not suppose that he will receive anything from the Lord, since he is a man of two minds, unstable in all his ways."

We must trust in Jesus and seek first the kingdom of God.

> Matthew 6:33 "But seek first the kingdom [of God] and his righteousness, and all these things will be given you besides."

One way of ascertaining whether or not you have surrendered to the Lord is to determine the extent to which you are living in your heart Matthew 5:6:

> "Blessed are they who hunger and thirst for righteousness,
> for they will be satisfied."

Most people don't know what the word "righteousness" means to them. Simply put, it is doing the will of the Father. Putting God first because we hunger for His will, grace and because we love Him with all our hearts, souls, minds and strength. When we strive for that surrender and have the love of God in our hearts, we find that the lack of forgiveness we have toward others and ourselves melts away. It truly is a blessing and miracle of the Lord!

The second key in fighting the battle against the enemy and sin is **asking for the release of the Holy Spirit in our lives**. At Baptism we are anointed "priest, prophet and king." When we "ask, we will receive, seek, we will find and knock, and the door will be opened."

> Luke 11: 11-13 "What father among you would hand his son a snake when he asks for a fish? Or hand him a scorpion when he asks for an egg? If you then, who are wicked, know how to give good gifts to your children, how much more will the Father in heaven give the holy Spirit to those who ask him?"

The Spirit is essential for fighting the battle against evil and any lack of forgiveness in our hearts. Ask now for the Holy Spirit to be released in your life!

The third essential is to **ask for faith**. When I ask people in my talks and seminars "how do we get faith or more faith?" most do not know the answer. The answer I hear the most is pray. That is partially true, but faith is a gift. We must ask for it and expect that we have received it.

> Ephesians 2:8 "For by grace you have been saved through faith, and this is not from you; it is the gift of God."

Having faith will dramatically change our lack of forgiveness and protect us from evil.

> 1 Peter 5:9 "Resist him, steadfast in faith knowing that your fellow believers throughout the world undergo the same sufferings."

When we have faith it acts as a shield against the attacks of the evil one.

Ephesians 6:16 "In all circumstances, hold faith as a shield, to quench all [the] flaming arrows of the evil one."

One of the saddest things for me is people not realizing that they are not just in a battle with a vicious enemy but an enemy who has been defeated by Jesus. We must realize that with God we have life and victory!

The fourth key essential to win the battle against evil and heal ourselves of the poison of not forgiving is to **use prayer and praise**. We know that the devil has to flee when we praise God. Additionally, it is important to pray for the Precious Blood of Jesus to cover ourselves and others. I often pray, "cover them with the Precious Blood of Jesus from the top of their hands to the bottom of their feet."

Praying in the "Spirit" is important also.

Ephesians 6:18 "With all prayer and supplication pray at every opportunity in the Spirit."

Use the gift of the Communion of Saints when you pray. Ask for the protection of Michael the Archangel, pray for his intercession, ask for the protection of the saints, your guardian angel, the Blessed Mother and ask for legions of angels to protect you. Finally, saying the name of Jesus is one of the most important things we can do to win this critical battle.

Luke 10:17 "Lord, even the demons are subject to us because of your name."

When we say the name of Jesus we use the power of the Lord.

Mark 16:17 "These signs will accompany those who believe: in my name they will drive out demons…"

God has given us **spiritual weapons to defeat the enemy**. This is the fifth step in our battle. The most important are the sacraments. Most of us don't realize the power of the Eucharist and the importance of receiving it on a daily basis. Another key sacrament is reconciliation. I can't emphasize this enough in our battle against lack of forgiveness and the enemy. I am often asked,

"How often should I go to confession?" The answer is when you are led by the Lord. For me, as someone who ministers to people, frequent reconciliation is necessary.

Reading Scripture and praying the rosary and the Divine Mercy Chaplet are also critical in our battle. Fasting is another important tool to give us strength and courage to persevere. Finally, don't be isolated. Find a prayer community and go to it often. We need the support of one another.

The sixth critical tactic in our battle against lack of forgiveness and evil is to **take every thought captive**.

> 2 Corinthians 10: 4-5 "For the weapons of our battle are not of flesh but are enormously powerful, capable of destroying fortresses. We destroy arguments and every pretension raising itself against the knowledge of God, and take every thought captive in obedience to Christ."

How do we do this? Philippians gives us the answer.

> Philippians 4:8 "Whatever is true, whatever is honorable, whatever is just, whatever is pure, whatever is lonely, whatever is gracious, if there is any excellence and if there is anything worthy of praise, think about these things."

Do not let anything enter your mind that is not of the Lord. Be careful about what you read, watch on television and look at on the internet. There is much sin our lives because of lack of disciple in what we let enter our minds.

The final key element in our battle is to **prioritize helping others and building the kingdom of God**. To what extent do you use your gifts and talents to help others and your parish? How are you making a difference in ministering to others? When your focus is trying to help others, your lack of forgiveness will melt away.

In summary, we are in a fierce battle against evil. Lack of forgiveness is one of the key evils to get out of our hearts. There are seven important steps to help you in your fight:

Totally surrender your heart and soul to Jesus.

Ask for the Baptism of the Holy Spirit.

Ask the Lord for more faith.

Use prayer, praise and the Name of Jesus often.

Take advantage of spiritual weapons: Mass and the Eucharist, reconciliation, rosary, Divine Mercy Chaplet, prayer groups and fasting.

Take every thought captive. Do not entertain evil in your mind.

Take your ministry seriously. God has given you special gifts to help build up the kingdom of God. Use them and the evil in your life will diminish or depart.

The battle against evil must be won. Ask the Lord to give you the wisdom and gifts you need to eradicate lack of forgiveness in your life. God bless you always!

CHAPTER 14
FORGIVENESS THROUGH THE PURSUIT OF HOLINESS

Scripture is clear. We are to pursue holiness.

> 1 Peter 1:15-16 "But as he who called you is holy, be holy yourselves in every aspect of your conduct, for it is written, 'be holy because I [am] holy.'"

Mother Teresa was poignant in her writings and would say that we must desire holiness and seek it with all our heart.

An important question for you: how can you be holy if you have animosity and lack of forgiveness in your hearts? If you have hatred or animosity toward another person, are you holy? We need to live in forgiveness and peace and we will truly be the light of Christ.

> Hebrews 12:14 "Strive for peace with everyone, and for that holiness without which no one will see the Lord."

When I bring up to people whether or not they are holy or are striving to be holy, they look at me like I am crazy. It is something they don't think about, let alone attempt to achieve. Why not? A big part of it is people don't hear teachings on holiness. They believe it is not necessary and most are sure it is impossible. It is such an error in thinking.

> 2 Timothy 1:9 "He saved us and called us to a holy life, not according to our works but according to his own design and the grace bestowed on us in Christ Jesus before time began."

Please take time to meditate on this Scripture. "He saved us and called us to a holy life." His death on the Cross, the pain He suffered, was to save us and allow us the opportunity to make a decision: do I truly want to be holy? Yes, it is not easy but consider the part that Jesus played. Do you want to waste the opportunity to be holy when our Savior did what He did to make us holy?

We have been set apart from others because of the love of the Lord. We are the adopted sons and daughters of God, bought with a price and anointed with the Blood of the Lamb.

> Leviticus 20:26 "To me, therefore, you shall be holy; for I, the LORD, am holy, and I have set you apart from other peoples to be my own."

We have been set free from sin and truly became free of our bondage. Now free, we have a decision to make: will we take advantage of our freedom and give back to the Lord what He desires? Do we want to be the personification of the love and the embodiment of love in action?

> Romans 6:22 "But now that you have been freed from sin and have become slaves of God, the benefit that you have leads to sanctification, and its end is eternal life."

Do you want to be holy? Does holding on to your lack of forgiveness mean more to you than being holy? When we don't forgive, it is like telling Jesus you don't care that He died on the Cross for you.

We are called to be the light of Christ: to live the Lord's Prayer and to forgive as we are forgiven. We are called to be perfect.

> Matthew 5:48 "So be perfect, just as your heavenly Father is perfect."

When we make a decision to be holy, God will take us up on it. God will do whatever it takes to remove anything in our lives preventing us from holiness. I received that "wake-up" call when I felt called by the Blessed Mother to go to France, first to Paris and then Lourdes. In the Church of the Miraculous Metal, I was praying and suddenly I heard a voice in my mind that I knew was not me: "I give you the gift of poverty."

I was so troubled that I quickly went to the back of the church, shaking badly. I prayed and looked up and said, "Really?" However, I did not want to be like the rich man who was called to give it all to the poor and did not. I prayed and told God, "If you want it, take it all."

I thought that it was my finances and money that I was to give to the Lord. I soon found out the error of my ways. The gift of "blessed are the poor in spirit" is to make God first and give Him everything in your life. Truly make Him the Lord of your life. This means your family, job, children, health, money … everything!

I began to experience a cleansing in my life. Forgiveness was a big part of it. I was to forgive others, which included my father, and people who deserted or betrayed me. I developed sciatica that was so bad that I couldn't stand for more than a few minutes at a time. What made it particularly challenging is that I was in sales and on my feet most of the day. It also was shocking because I had just became a deacon and had to stand behind the altar for what seemed like an eternity. People who were watching me said it looked like I was going to pass out because of the pain.

I was fired from my job as Senior Vice President of Sales from a Fortune 25 company. I was recognized two months earlier as one of the top executives in the world, out of 20,000 employees. What changed? The previous CEO and I had a great relationship, but he retired. The new CEO didn't like me and wanted to bring in his own person. What also changed is that the Lord was cleansing anything that I prioritized ahead of Him. I had to forgive the people who were involved in firing me. That was not easy. I needed a "miracle." I needed God's supernatural intervention and grace to be able to forgive. I ascertained later that without my being fired, I probably would never have become a deacon. I was weighed down with restricted stock and stock options and it was unlikely that I would have left my job in New Jersey. When I came back a few months later, I was asked to become a deacon. This is how God works. He removes things in our lives that are barriers to holiness.

Family was a god to me. Coming from an Italian heritage, the closeness of family—such things as having the Sunday meal together—was a top priority. Much of that changed when my daughter decided to go off on her own without us. Unbelievably painful. For years we were in disarray. God was telling me to rely on Him. He was my family. Once I put Him first, everything changed with my family and we had forgiveness for one another.

Desiring to achieve holiness is everything. Ask for it, desire it, seek it with all your heart and consecrate yourself to the Lord as sweet incense.

Leviticus 20: 7-8 "Sanctify yourselves,

then, and be holy: for I the LORD, your God, am holy. Be careful, therefore, to observe my statutes. I, the LORD, make you holy."

What does it mean to "sanctify" ourselves? It is to think and act differently than how the world teaches us.

One of the most important aspects of becoming holy is to examine your conscience on a daily basis. When you have sin in your life, eliminate it. That starts with prayer and being led by the Lord so you can understand why you are turning away from God and turning to sin. It is critical that you get before the Lord in silence. Confirm your struggles to Him and let Him love you. Also, let your Lord lead you to repentance and reconciliation. I am convinced that frequent reconciliation is a requirement for holiness. It is through reconciliation that we find forgiveness of our sins, ourselves and others who we struggle to forgive.

I am also convinced that we can't receive the holiness we must have without frequent and, in most cases, daily Mass. We need the Body and Blood of our Lord to flow through us and heal us of everything that separates us from Him. Do you ever notice how your day and attitude gets better when you go to Mass? Everything changes when you make it a priority. It might take a while before you notice a difference, but you will see a huge change over time when you go to daily Mass.

In addition to the sacraments, desire holiness through faith. Why is faith so important?

> Hebrews 11:6, "But without faith it is impossible to please him, for anyone who approaches God must believe that he exists and that he rewards those who seek him."

We know that holiness pleases God. If that is true, then strong faith must be at the core of holiness. It is transforming places in the world such as Africa leading to vocations and a transformation of hearts and minds.

We have discussed the importance of praise. When we praise the Lord, we release holiness within our soul. It is praise that opens the door to act in holiness with our interactions with other people. It is praise that helps change our attitudes into one of forgiveness of others.

When we are in a state of holiness we absolutely want to pray. This, after we praise and worship, also leads us to intercessory prayer. Praying the rosary and the Divine Mercy Chaplet is important to our development of personal holiness. God is always looking for people who are warriors for Him who "stand in the gap" by praying for the holiness and healing of His people. Make a list of the people who the Lord wants you to pray for. Pray a decade of the rosary for each member of your family or a bead for each person on your list. You will never regret being an intercessor for God's people. Often your prayers will be used to bring people away from sin and move toward Christ. I believe that we will never realize how much our prayers bore fruit until we are with the Lord in heaven.

When we are in a state of holiness, we feel the love of the Lord. We want to share that love with other people. We meditate on how much God loves us and we tell others that they are loved. We also want to serve Him by living the acts of mercy of helping those who need our assistance in any way.

How do you spend your time? I see so many

people who focus on pleasing themselves through sports, vacations, watching television and countless other things. Are these things bad for us? Of course not. However, there is only so much time we have. We can go through life trying to experience pleasure or we can make a commitment to prioritize our time to serve God and His people.

I often get questioned why I do the things I do. Instead of vacations, I go on mission trips or lead people on pilgrimages. Instead of time at the beach, I am giving talks and seminars. The important thing is to pray and ask the Lord what He wants you to do. Don't compare yourself with other people and what they are doing or not doing. At times, you may look at people and say "I am doing more than them." However, they may not be doing much of anything.

I have found that any hardness of heart disappears quickly when I am serving the Lord and His people. I feel the Lord's presence and holiness when I am serving others and not just myself.

Our goal in life must be to be holy. When we strive for holiness, the lack of forgiveness in our lives simply goes away because we realize that God is love and He wants us to love others with that love, no matter what they have done to us.

CHAPTER 15
MARY AND FORGIVENESS

We are blessed! We are blessed because we have a God who has created us in His image, who loves us unconditionally and gave us His only Son, Jesus, who died and rose again so that we may have eternal life. We are also blessed because we have been given a spiritual mother who loves us and wants to intercede for us and bring us closer to her Son Jesus.

Mary is described as the "Mother of Mercy," but Pope Francis, in the Year of Mercy, described Mary also as the "Mother of forgiveness." He recited the words of an ancient hymn: "Hail Mother of mercy, Mother of God, Mother of forgiveness, Mother of hope, Mother of grace and Mother of holy gladness." He went on to elucidate that for generations we have sought her intercession and consolation.

Pope Francis explained how critical it was to understand "forgiveness." The pope went on: "A person unable to forgive has not yet known the fullness of love. Only one who truly loves is able to forgive and forget. At the foot of the Cross, Mary becomes for all people the mother of forgiveness, as she follows in the example of her Son who forgives those who are killing him."

The pope further explains, "For us, Mary is an icon of how the Church must offer forgiveness to those who seek it. The Mother of forgiveness teaches the Church that the forgiveness granted on Golgotha knows no limits. Neither the law with its quibbles, nor the wisdom of this world with its distinctions, can hold it back. The Church's forgiveness must be every bit as broad as that offered by Jesus on the Cross and by Mary at his feet. There is no other way."

We are blessed, according to Pope Francis, because Mary offers us a "three-fold gift of her son: hope, grace and holy gladness. The gift that Mary bestows in offering us Jesus is the forgiveness which renews life, enables us once more to do God's will and fills us with true happiness. This grace frees the heart to look to the future with the joy born of hope."

The pontiff emphasized the importance of forgiveness as "the true antidote to the sadness caused by resentment and vengeance by bringing peace and serenity by freeing the heart from resentment."

We were told by the pope, "let us allow her to lead us to the rediscovery of the beauty of an encounter with her Son Jesus. Let us open wide the doors of our heart to the joy of forgiveness, conscious that we have been given new confidence and hope, and thus make our daily lives a humble instrument of God's love."

We were told by Jesus on the Cross to "behold our Mother." Doesn't a mother want the best for us? What mother would want us harboring poison in our souls by failing to forgive? Our spiritual Mother stands and watches us, interceding as we go through our own cross. She is ever vigilant as she unconditionally loves us, always watching and interceding for our intentions. She greatly desires us to repent of our sins and lack of forgiveness, and to love God with all our heart and soul.

Do we believe that our Mother's intercession can lead to miracles in our lives? Especially miracles of forgiveness and softening of our hearts? We see the example of how Mary goes to her Son Jesus and asks Him for a miracle: "they ran out of wine." Mary is our spiritual mother and needs to be an integral part of our faith life and spirituality.

We learn from Hebrews that only through faith can we truly please our Lord Jesus. Mary is the perfect example of the personification of faith. When the angel Gabriel appeared to her, she never doubted that it was going to happen. She showed tremendous faith in Luke 1:38:

> "Behold, I am the handmaid of the Lord. May it be done to me according to your word."

This complete faith and trust had Mary believing the angel's proclamation that her cousin Elizabeth was with child in her sixth month. This led Mary to take the long and difficult trip at a young age to see Elizabeth.

We read and meditate on Mary's faith and it helps us understand that to get closer to Jesus we must be clean of heart and not have any animosity or lack of forgiveness in our hearts.

> Matthew 5:8 "Blessed are the clean of heart,

> for they will see God."

My brothers and sisters, how can we be clean of heart if we are holding onto our hurts, wounds and pain and fail to forgive?

When we forgive, we can emulate the words of Mary in Luke 1:46:

> "My soul proclaims the greatness of the Lord;

> my spirit rejoices in God my savior."

When Jesus fills our heart we want to shout it from the rooftops. We no longer have the bitterness of refusing to forgive in our hearts but are filled with love and joy.

Our Blessed Mother is at the center of forgiveness and healing. For some of us, we feel it is nearly impossible for us to forgive ourselves or others who have hurt us. Where there is great healing, there is Mary. We can feel her presence as she intercedes for us through her Son Jesus. We see so many miracles at Lourdes, Fatima and at other Marian shrines throughout the world. Draw upon her love and intercession to pray for healing of forgiveness and other forms of healing. The love of our mother adds in the realization of Mark 11:23:

> "Amen, I say to you, whoever says to this mountain, 'Be lifted up and thrown into the sea,' and does not doubt in his heart but believes that what he says will happen, it shall be done for him. Therefore, I tell you, all that you ask for in prayer, believe you will receive it and it shall be yours."

There was a man paralyzed in the hospital who was told that he would never walk again. He had not forgiven himself or God. He hadn't been to church for 30 years. I reminded him how much God and the Blessed Mother loved him and how he was forgiven and to forgive himself, the church and others who needed to be forgiven. He had never learned how to pray the rosary. Once he learned, he was joyous in praying the mysteries. A week later he began to move what was once paralyzed. Several weeks later he was totally healed and walking. Praise God! Great miracles occur through the love and forgiveness of Jesus and the intercession of Mary!

In the Blessed Mother's six appearances at Fatima, she encouraged the children to pray the rosary. The rosary is a tremendous gift to help us forgive and intercede for others. In her third appearance to the shepherd children, Mary told them: "Sacrifice yourself for sinners, and say many times, especially whenever you make some sacrifice, 'O my Jesus, it is for the love of Thee for the conversion of sinners, and in reparation for the sins committed against the Immaculate Heart of Mary.'" Additionally, Mary taught us as our Lady of Fatima to pray at the end of each decade of the rosary, "O my Jesus, forgive us our sins, save us from the fire of hell, take all souls to heaven, especially those in most need of your mercy."

Peace and forgiveness are two sides of the same coin. They go together because when we forgive, we receive the fruit of the Spirit which includes having peace in our hearts. The fruit of peace is a message from Our Lady everywhere she has appeared. It was the third part of her Fatima message. She spoke to the children often about peace and urged them to pray for peace. This occurred during World War I, a time of tremendous destruction and loss of life in Europe. Additionally, Mary told all of us to do penance and pray for peace because otherwise men will perish. She gave the children a vision of hell and told them to pray for urgent peace, to fight for peace and plead to God for peace.

Do you have struggles with forgiveness? If you do, and most of us do, then pray for peace and expect miracles in your life. Jesus told us in John 14:27:

> "Peace I leave with you; my peace I give to you. Not as the world gives do I give it to you."

He also emphasized in the Beatitudes:

> Matthew 5:9 "Blessed are the peacemakers,
>
> for they will be called children of God."

Our attitude will determine our peace and our forgiveness.

> Philippians 4:4-9 "Rejoice in the Lord

always. I shall say it again; rejoice! Your kindness should be known to all. The Lord is near. Have no anxiety at all, but in everything, by prayer and petition, with thanksgiving, make your requests known to God. Then the peace of God that surpasses all understanding will guard your hearts and minds in Christ Jesus.

"Finally brothers, whatever is true, whatever is honorable, whatever is just, whatever is pure, whatever is lovely, whatever is gracious, if there is any excellence and if there is anything worthy of praise, think about these things. Keep on doing what you have learned and received and heard and seen in me. Then the God of peace will be with you."

To receive forgiveness in our lives we also need to obtain the "hope" that Mary tells us about in her messages. Hope is fundamental to forgiveness. Jesus will give us hope because He is the God of hope.

Romans 15:13 "May the God of hope fill you with all joy and peace in believing, so that you may abound in hope by the power of the holy Spirit."

When we have faith it leads to hope for the future. We walk by faith and not by sight which gives us hope in our lives. Our Mother, who is Queen of the Angels, is interceding for us in our battle for forgiveness. She calls upon the angels, especially our guardian angel, to intercede for us. Do you fear you will never forgive what needs to be forgiven? Ask for more faith and surrender your heart to Jesus and seek the peace and hope that only Jesus can give us.

In my life, I have found that our Mother can lead us to want to forgive, even in the most difficult situations. There are people who are difficult to forgive. Ask our Mother, who is "full of grace," to intercede and give you strength to forgive. There have been people who have betrayed my trust and said things that were not true. Jesus had the same problem.

When we are wronged, we can harbor ill will or choose to forgive those who have hurt us. We all know forgiveness is difficult or even impossible. However, God is the God of the possible. It is through His grace and the intercession of our spiritual Mother that the miracle of forgiveness can occur.

So many people do not have a relationship or devotion to Mary. They miss an opportunity for a deeper spiritual life and love of Jesus. Pray the rosary every day and pray for those who you are struggling to forgive. When you do, your life will change dramatically for the better. Praise God and expect great miracles of forgiveness!

CHAPTER 16
FORGIVENESS AND FAITH

Faith is the foundation of our relationship with Jesus. As mentioned in Hebrews 11:6, it is impossible to please God without faith. Faith is mentioned in the Bible over 200 times. It is faith that moves mountains. It is faith that will give you the strength to forgive, even in the most difficult of circumstances.

Nearly every saint in history has had dark moments and moments of despair. Mother Teresa, in her letters to confessors and confidants, revealed many challenging times of travail. She wrote, "I have no faith, I dare not utter the words and thoughts that crowd in my heart and make me suffer untold agony." She even said her constant smile was a "mask or cloak that covers everything." Perhaps you feel that way now. To the world everything is wonderful but inside you feel darkness, hopelessness and despair. Saint Therese of Lisieux described her doubt as a "night of nothingness."

Our suffering is part of our journey for increased faith and gives us the strength to forgive ourselves and others. We know that God is molding and perfecting us in His image. We are being shaped by the fire of the Holy Spirit in our hearts and souls.

> 1 Peter 1:6-7 "In this you rejoice, although now for a little while you may have to suffer through various trials, so that the genuineness of your faith, more precious than gold that is perishable even though tested by fire, may prove to be for praise, glory, and honor at the revelation of Jesus Christ."

All the suffering, doubt, fear and lack of forgiveness can and will be used by Christ to increase our faith. However, it is up to us to say "yes" to our molding by Christ into ambassadors of love and forgiveness.

Often we know we should forgive, we want to forgive, but we don't have the faith to forgive. We think that things will get worse if we forgive those who have hurt us. The essence of this dilemma is fear, fear that we will be seen to be weak to ourselves and others and be taken advantage of to our dismay. However, fear and lack of forgiveness is never bigger than God's love.

> 1 John 4:18 "There is no fear in love, but perfect love drives out fear because fear has to do with punishment, and so one who fears is not yet perfect in love."

We have to always remember that God is love.

> 1 John 4:16 "God is love, and whoever remains in love remains in God and God in him."

To be healed of our lack of forgiveness, we must increase our love and faith. In order to do that, we must plead for God's mercy and ask for more faith and love. Do we believe without seeing or are we like the Apostle Thomas? Do we have the faith of the centurion? Do we believe that our prayers will make a difference in our ability to forgive?

One of the most important aspects of our spiritual growth is to pray and expect that God hears us and wants to bless us with more faith. If we pray and expect the miracle of faith, we can be assured that we will get it!

> James 1: 5-8 "If any of you lacks wisdom, he should ask God who gives to all generously and ungrudgingly, and he will be given it. But he should ask in faith, not doubting, for the one who doubts is like a wave of the sea that is driven and tossed about by the wind. For that person must not suppose that he will receive anything from the Lord since he is a man of two minds, unstable in his ways."

By learning how to pray and ask for faith we learn to live this Scripture:

> 2 Corinthians 5:7 "We walk by faith, not by sight."

This faith will enable us to forgive and heal ourselves of the poison of animosity, grudges and lack of forgiveness, and transform our lives forever to receive the blessings that God has in store for us. Think of how long you have had this pain of not forgiving someone or yourself. Isn't it time to change our behavior and finally get peace in our hearts? Pray for the miracle that God wants to give you!

> Mark 11:24 "Therefore, I tell you, all that you ask for in prayer, believe you will receive it and it shall be yours."

> 1 John 5: 14-15 "We have this confidence in him, that if we ask anything according to his will, he hears us. And if we know that he hears us in regard to whatever we ask, we know that what we have asked him for is ours."

How much do we believe that God will heal us of our lack of forgiveness? Do we have the faith that God's promises will come into our hearts? There were two blind men who heard that Jesus was a healer and called out to Jesus when He was passing by them.

> Matthew 9:27-30 "Two blind men followed [Jesus], crying out, 'Son of David, have pity on us!' … Jesus said to them, 'Do you believe that I can do this?'

'Yes, Lord,' they said to him. Then he touched their eyes and said, 'Let it be done for you according to your faith.' And their eyes were opened.'"

This Scripture is extremely important in our striving for holiness. How big is our God? Do you feel that God is more powerful than the stronghold of our lack of forgiveness? Do we expect miracles in our lives? Do we have the faith to move the mountain of our emotional pain?

Matthew 17:20 "If you have faith the size of a mustard seed, you will say to this mountain, 'Move from here to there,' and it will move. Nothing will be impossible for you."

I have been blessed in my life and ministry to see many miracles through having faith. One in particular was very impactful to me. We were on a pilgrimage to the Holy Land and with us was a woman with a dislocated shoulder. The injury had occurred just the day before the trip, but she still wanted to go. I knew God wanted to do a miracle with her. On the second day on the trip, the Lord came to me in front of one of the churches and told me to pray for her and that He would heal her. I asked her the question that Jesus asked the blind men: "do you believe that Jesus can heal you?" I will never forget what she said and how she said it. She looked at me, paused, her eyes widened and she almost shouted, "I do believe!" I then prayed fervently over her shoulder for about 30 seconds. I could see in her face how much she believed. She looked at me and suddenly, with an arm that previously couldn't be lifted above her waist, raised it above her head and started shouting, "Alleluia, Alleluia, Alleluia!" Praise God! Now and forever! Another miracle for the Lord!

Yes, God does physical miracles, but how about emotional miracles and miracles of forgiveness? Is it possible to begin loving someone who has hurt us deeply and who we have not forgiven? I wanted to forgive my father for his ignoring me, abusing me emotionally and hurting me physically.

I prayed fervently for the grace to forgive him. A critical part of the process was that I expected that God would give me the grace to forgive him and love him like I wanted to as his son. Another critical step was that I acted as if I had received this miracle of forgiveness even if at first I didn't feel like it. I began to see him regularly when he was bedridden and started loving him in a way that I had not done previously. The more that I performed loving acts of tenderness and forgiveness, the more that I actually forgave him. God was healing me of a deep wound!

None of this is easy. You need endurance and perseverance to do God's will and receive what He wants to give you.

> Hebrews 10: 35-36 "Therefore, do not throw away your confidence; it will have great recompense. You need endurance to do the will of God and receive what he has promised."

There will be so many times that you feel like giving up. Your emotional hurt is so deep that you don't think it is worth it. This is a lie of the enemy who wants to hold you in bondage. Freedom comes through forgiveness. It is the forgiveness of Jesus that has set up free of the bondage of sin.

It is extremely important that you stay the course and realize that God is healing you no matter whether or not the circumstances look like it. By faith we know that all things work for good.

> Romans 8:28 "We know that all things work for good for those who love God, who are called according to his purpose."

God uses everything in our lives to shape and mold us and bring us closer to Him.

Do not give up! God's blessings are right around the corner. There is so much pain and suffering when we are in a relationship that has turned to bitterness and even hatred. God's love is there to heal our wounds and heal us of our lack of forgiveness. He will never abandon us.

> Romans 8: 35, 37-39 "What will separate us from the love of Christ? Will anguish, or distress, or persecution, or famine, or nakedness, or peril, or the sword? No, in all these things we conquer overwhelming through him who loved us. For I am convinced that neither death, nor life, nor angels, nor principalities, nor present things, nor future things, nor powers, nor height, nor depth, nor any other creature will be able to separate us from the love of God in Christ Jesus our Lord."

To forgive takes faith but it also takes a different

attitude. A significant part of that attitude is listening. We are given two ears and one mouth. We should be listening twice as much as we talk. For many of us the reverse is true! Could it be that part of the reason we have relationships that are strained or even totally ruptured is because we don't really listen to the other person?

To listen fervently and have "active" listening is hard to accomplish. One of the challenges is that we think in our minds at a rate of 750 words per minute and most of us speak at a rate of 150 to 250 words a minute. If we think up to five times faster than the words spoken to us, what fills up the gap? We start thinking of a myriad of subjects that distract us from what the person is trying to communicate to us: what we are doing later, things we have to get done, that we're bored or daydreaming, etc. Whatever it is, it doesn't help us understand the meaning behind the words being spoken to us. That leads to misunderstanding and having the person speaking feeling not valued or appreciated.

Good listening skills are an art. One of the keys to understanding what the person is truly trying to communicate is to learn how to "read" body language. It is nonverbal communication that psychologists tell us represents 65% of all communication. When someone looks away from you it tells you that there is an issue. If they put a hand over their mouth they have a problem with what is being said. We should stop and ask them their opinion. If they step back, they may not agree. When they "steeple" their fingers they believe that they are in a position of authority. Take the time to do some research and learn the clues of nonverbal communication. The most important thing to remember is that it is the change of nonverbal communication that is the most significant part of active listening. When someone depicts a problem their facial expressions will change and they will signal it. Instead of speaking, listen to their opinions!

While 65% of communication is nonverbal, 28% is the tone of our speaking. Listen to the words that are emphasized. The most important part of the tone of communication is the pace and pitch of it. Does the speaker raise their voice over certain words? Do they pause before key words or phrases? All of this is critical to ascertaining what people are trying to communicate.

It is shocking to most of us to understand that only 7% of our communication is the actual words we say. What is even more amazing is that we only retain 20% of what is said to us at any given time and within 24 hours it is down to 10%. No wonder we feel misunderstood and not listened to in our relationships!

To better communicate, use every tool of listening and communication to strength our relationships. Use positive nonverbal communication. Move toward the person when speaking, but do not invade their space. Look at them in their eyes when you are speaking, but equally important, when they are speaking to us! Do not change nonverbal communication by putting your hands over your mouth or face or folding your arms when you disagree with what you are hearing. Smile fervently and be warm and loving as best you can. When you do this, the lack of forgiveness between you and others will diminish dramatically!

We know that damaged relationships usually involve both parties doing things that are harmful and hurtful. Take responsibility for your actions and things said that hurt the relationship. Ask for forgiveness and apply the gift of humility. This is true even if you feel that the other person is much more at fault.

God wants you to live a life of holiness, abundance and joy. When you are healed of your issues with forgiveness, you are well on the way! It takes faith to believe that God is healing you and your relationships. Ask for the faith that moves mountains and transforms relationships and expect miracles!

CHAPTER 17
FORGIVENESS AND
SACRAMENTAL LIFE

All of us are sinners and desperately need forgiveness. It is one of the most important aspects of our lives; we need and must have supernatural grace and forgiveness. We need the miracle of forgiveness from God! We don't have the power to forgive others and to forgive ourselves in a way that will heal us. When we open our hearts to receive God's forgiveness, it changes our ability to forgive others.

How do we transform our hearts to receive the forgiveness that God wants to give us? It is through the Sacrament of Reconciliation.

Confession is an incredible act of love in which we enter stained and sinful and leave white as snow. Meditate on the love that God pours into us. We enter the confessional often full of shame and leave with peace and hope.

It is critical that each of us individually embrace humility. To go to confession is an act of humility, especially when we go to a priest who we know well. Reconciliation is humility in action! It is through humility that we embrace love and this sacrament of forgiveness.

Confession is the sacrament that can mold us into an image of Christ. It is the mercy, sacrifice and forgiveness which transforms our character. If there is anything that separates us from Jesus, this sacrament will bring us together. We allow God to take away anything that is poison for our souls.

Throughout this book, we have described lack of forgiveness as a poison that enters us and pollutes our spirituality. How many times do we enter the confessional with the idea of confessing how we have not forgiven various people in our lives? The reality of the sin of not forgiving someone needs to be confessed. It is important to remember that we are sinners and we must go to confession as sinners, to tell God we are sorry for what we have done that may have hurt Him.

Before we go to confession, we should pray and allow the Lord to reveal to us our sins, including our lack of forgiveness, and so that we may be sorry for our sins. We should ask for grace to overcome habitual sin and temptations and increase personal virtue and our love of God.

Penance is absolutely necessary to help train us to forgive others and ourselves. It is through penance and discipline that we learn how to tame the unholy passions and desires that attack us. Through the process of confession and penance we strive for the fruit of the Holy Spirit rather than the pleasure of the flesh.

To reverse many years of struggling to forgive, we need the sacraments to give us the strength to transform our behavior. We must hunger to be one with Jesus through the Sacrament of Reconciliation and the Mass and Holy Eucharist. After I go to confession, I feel like I am walking on air! I can feel the Father's arms around me as I say "Abba," daddy!

God's mercy is greater than anything we can

imagine! When we sin or harbor lack of forgiveness we can go to the Father and sincerely say, "I'm sorry and I repent." God is a forgiving Father and you can be assured that He will forgive us.

It takes a great deal of courage to break the bondage of sin and lack of forgiveness. It is through humility that we can go to confession and receive God's forgiveness. What happens if we go to confession and then find ourselves sinning soon afterward? It is more than okay to go back to reconciliation if you need the help and grace.

One of the most important spiritual disciplines for us to learn is examination of our conscience on a daily basis. Go before the Lord for your prayer time, perhaps in the evening. Ask the Lord to reveal to you when you have chosen sin instead of the Lord. When you have moved away from Him, called desolation, rather than toward Him, called consolation. This exercise is like a reflective mirror to examine our motivation with our actions. It is through this discipline that we can dig deep into our souls and attempt to ascertain what the stumbling blocks are that usually are connected to some type of forgiveness issue.

Knowledge of ourselves is a critical part of spiritual awareness and growth. While I am far from a saint, I can relate to so many of them who saw themselves as wicked and wretched. It is critical to truly pray and meditate and taste the love, mercy and forgiveness of God; it is hard not to see ourselves as horrible.

When we see our sin and weakness, we are on the way to greater holiness. If we see ourselves as people who don't need mercy and forgiveness, we will only get deeper into sin and not forgive others of their weaknesses. Reconciliation begins with a desire for a clean heart, which will help us see God in ourselves and others.

Once we have gone and become clean through the Sacrament of Reconciliation, we are now ready to unite with Christ through the Eucharist. It is the love of Jesus that gives us the Eucharist, which is mandatory for us to achieve holiness and be the personification of God's love and forgiveness. Our souls must be one with Christ and the Eucharist.

Jesus is clear on the importance of the "bread of life."

> John 6: 51 "I am the living bread that came down from heaven; whoever eats this bread will live forever; and the bread that I will give is my flesh for the life of the world."

How important is this for us? It is essential in our battle of forgiveness of ourselves and others.

> John 6: 53-56 "Jesus said to them, 'Amen, amen, I say to you, unless you eat the flesh of the Son of Man and drink his blood, you do not have life within you. Whoever eats my flesh and drinks my blood has eternal life and I will raise him on the last day. For my flesh is true food, and my blood is true drink. Whoever eats my flesh and drinks my blood remains in me and I in him.'"

Our life is connected to our willingness to be connected with the Eucharist and have it be an integral part of our lives. Jesus tells us over and over that He "thirsts." He is hungry for souls and for us individually. Jesus wants us to forgive so that He can fill us with His love, forgiveness and grace. Jesus is constantly saying "come to me." When we come to Him we want to forgive and be healed. We can no longer harbor bitterness and a spirit of holding onto our lack of forgiveness.

When we receive Holy Communion we need to do it with a heart that is free of hatred or anything that is against the love that is God. The Eucharist is the intimate union with Jesus into our body and soul in an unique way. In reading books on the saints, we find that many spent hours in preparation and thanksgiving before they received His Body and Blood.

Our ability to truly eradicate our lack of forgiveness is to ask the Lord to wash away our sins and cleanse us of sin and any animosity in our hearts and souls. Jesus is the "Bread of Life." It is this bread which truly transforms us into agents of His love, joy and peace. Jesus wanted to give Himself to us in a way that was necessary for our spiritual union and growth.

There are times in our lives when we feel broken, not wanted, unloved and lonely. In Isaiah 43:4, God tells us how important we are to Him:

> "Because you are precious in my eyes
> and honored, and I love you."

We are so important that He humbles Himself and

allows Himself to be held in our hands as His Body and Blood.

The sacraments give us strength when we need it most, which is most of the time. We need to trust in Jesus and not be afraid to turn to Him.

> Isaiah 41: 10,13 "Do not fear: I am with you;
>
> do not be anxious: I am your God.
>
> I will strengthen you, I will help you,
>
> I will uphold you with my victorious right hand.
>
> "… For I am the LORD your God,
>
> who grasp your right hand;
>
> It is I who say to you, Do not fear,
>
> I will help you."

It is so critical to fully grasp how much Jesus wants us to be transformed into His image of love and forgiveness. That is why forgiveness is so emphasized as being paramount to being forgiven by God. Jesus calls us each by name and delivers us from the evil one.

Isaiah 43: 1-2, "Do not fear, for I have redeemed you;

I have called you by name: you are mine.

When you pass through waters, I will be with you;

through rivers, you shall not be swept away.

When you walk through fire, you shall not be burned,

nor will flames consume you."

It is time we make a decision to forgive and be one with Jesus. If you are reading this book, it is because God wants to heal you. When you are healed of your issues with forgiveness you can then be used to be an instrument of peace. Your desire to live a life of love and forgiveness will be brand new. We can truly experience the Lord saying to us that we are a new creation in Him. We can hear Jesus saying to us, "Behold, I make all things new!"

There is no substitute for making reconciliation and daily Mass an integral part of our lives. It is so vital that it is the same as making sure you have daily food, drink and sleep. Jesus loves you passionately and has forgiven you. Connect with Him through the sacraments and live a life of abundance!

CHAPTER 18
EMPOWERED AND SENT

God loves you so much, I can almost feel His heart aching for you to say "yes" to Him! He wants you to move away from bitterness and apathy into a relationship of love with Him and spread that love to others. When you are on that road, everything changes. You want to make a difference and serve Him. You want to use your gifts and talents.

I believe that meditating on the two parables and story of the Last Judgment in Matthew 25 can be life-changing. It offers three incredible lessons to teach us about the urgency of using our talents to serve our brothers and sisters. The first parable is about the ten virgins. They took their lamps to meet the Bridegroom, who was delayed. Five were wise, but five were foolish because they brought no oil for their lamps. In other words, the five foolish virgins were not prepared. When the Bridegroom finally came, they were sent out to buy oil. It was too late!

> Matthew 25: 10-13 "While they went off to buy it, the bridegroom came and those who were ready went into the wedding feast with him. Then the door was locked. Afterwards the other virgins came and said, 'Lord, Lord, open the door for us!' But he said in reply, 'Amen, I say to you, I do not know you.' Therefore, stay awake, for you know neither the day or the hour."

What does this parable mean to you personally? If Jesus called you to Him now, would you be ready? Have your gifts been used by Jesus to build the Body of Christ? Some theologians believe we will be asked one question by Jesus after we die, "Who did you bring with you?" This parable is so important for us not to delay using our gifts but to look for opportunities to use them for Jesus and the Body of Christ.

The second parable is one of my favorites, the Parable of the Talents. A man was going on a journey and called to his servants and "entrusted his possessions to them."

Matthew 25: 15-30 "To one he gave five talents, to another two; to a third, one—to each according to his ability. Then he went away. Immediately the one who received five talents went and traded with them, and made another five. Likewise, the one who received two made another two. But the man who received one went and dug a hole in the ground and buried his master's money. After a long time the master of those servants came back and settled accounts with them. The one who had received five talents came forward bringing the additional five. He said, 'Master, you gave me five talents. See, I have made five more.' His master said to him, 'Well done, my good and faithful servant. Since you were faithful in small matters, I will give you great responsibilities. Come share your master's joy.' [Then] the one who had received two talents also came forward and said, 'Master, you gave me two talents. See, I have made two more.' His master said to him, 'Well done, my good and faithful servant. Since you were faithful in small matters, I will give you great responsibilities. Come, share your master's joy.' Then the one who had received the one talent came forward and said, 'Master, I knew you were a demanding person, harvesting where you did not plant and gathering where you did not scatter; so out of fear I went off and buried your talent in the ground. Here it is back.' His master said to him in reply, 'You wicked, lazy servant! So you knew that I harvest where I did not plant and gather where I did not scatter? Should you not then have put my money in the bank that I could have got it back with interest on my return? Now then! Take the talent from him and give it to the one with ten. For to everyone who has, more will be given and he will grow rich; but from the one who has not, even what he has will be taken away. And throw this useless servant into the darkness outside, where there will be wailing and grinding of teeth.'"

I think about this parable all the time. Each of us has been given spiritual gifts for the good of the Body of Christ. The question is: are we aware of our gifts? Do we pray for God to reveal them to us?

> 1 Corinthians 12: 4-12 "There are different kinds of spiritual gifts but the same Spirit; there are different forms of service but the same Lord; there are different workings but the same God who produces all of them in everyone. To each individual the manifestation of the Spirit is given for some benefit. To one is given the Spirit the expression of wisdom; to another the expression of knowledge according to the same Spirit; to another faith by the same Spirit; to another gifts of healing by the one Spirit; to another mighty deeds; to another prophecy; to another discernment of spirits; to another varieties of tongues; to another interpretation of tongues. But one and the same Spirit produces all of these, distributing them individually to

each person as he wishes."

My dream and earnest desire is to be used to build up the Body of Christ. I know that when we don't forgive, we are paralyzed and it is difficult to be used in the way that God wants to use us. Everything starts with the desire to be used. I have often said in my talks that there is a direct ratio between the degree that we are used by God to minister to His people, and the amount we want to be used. Do we hunger and thirst to be used? Do we come up with countless excuses that we don't have time? It isn't the right time in my life? My spouse won't let me? I have too much on my plate? My work is too demanding? Someone else has more ability and talent? I don't have the skills? I think I have heard most of the excuses. This is what I know; God will make it happen when our heart is in the right place. If we sincerely want to be used then God will find a way to make it happen. Don't let sin or lack of forgiveness get in the way. Sometimes the very people who you have a hard time forgiving are the people you are supposed to work with and are the key to great miracles occurring!

Mother Teresa said that in the "judgment of the

nations" in Matthew 25, we get a glimpse of what Jesus will ask us when we get before Him.

> Matthew 25: 31-40 "When the Son of Man comes in his glory, and all the angels with him, he will sit upon his glorious throne, and all the nations will be assembled before him. And he will separate them one from another, as a shepherd separates the sheep from the goats. He will place the sheep on his right and the goats on his left. Then the king will say to those on his right, 'Come, you who are blessed by my Father, inherit the kingdom prepared for you from the foundation of the world. For I was hungry and you gave me food, I was thirty and you gave me drink, a stranger and you welcomed me, naked and you clothed me, ill and you cared for me, in prison and you visited me.' The righteous will answer him and say, 'Lord when did we see you hungry and feed you, or thirsty and give you drink? When did we see you a stranger and welcome you, or naked and clothe you? When did we see you ill or in prison, and visit you?'

And the king will say to them in reply, 'Amen, I say to you, whatever you did for one of these least brothers of mine, you did for me."

There are many people who read and/or hear this Scripture and say to themselves, "This is not for me. It is not my gift." Yet, it was directed to each of us individually. We are called to be Jesus to those who are abandoned, hurting and in pain. The people who are hungry are in the billions. We know the poor are all over the world. The question for each of us is: which of these poor people are we being called to minister to and meet their needs? I received three dreams telling me to minister to the poor in the Philippines, which also led to my working with the poor in Indonesia. People would question me intently as to why I felt so compelled to go to the Philippines and Indonesia. It was even more amazing when I realized that God was using us to support abandoned children in the Philippines, a school in the jungle of Indonesia and a church in the midst of the poorest of the poor in Manila. I was called and decided to act on the calling. Have you been called? If not, you soon will be!

John 15:16 "It was not you who chose me, but I who chose you and appointed you to go and bear fruit that will remain, so that whatever you ask the Father in my name he may give you."

Are there sick in your parish? Are some in the hospital? Of course there are! I am sure that most of us who have been in the hospital greatly appreciate those who took the time to come see us. If we felt loved by being visited by people when we are sick, we can be assured that others will appreciate our love when we see them, especially if we pray over them! I believe all of us are called to visit the sick. This also will be a grace to help us in our struggle with forgiving other people.

One of the greatest gifts we can give others and ourselves is to visit the incarcerated. I can't begin to tell you the satisfaction you will receive when you take the time to see those who often are in severe emotional pain. So many times those incarcerated feel worthless and that is there is nothing that they can do to please God. This is another lie of the devil. The reality is that God hears the cry of the poor and those behind bars who are often financially poor and always poor in spirit.

When you see those in prison, remind them who they are: children of God, loved unconditionally, and recipients of every spiritual blessing. Teach them how to pray the rosary and the Divine Mercy Chaplet, and tell them that their prayers of intercession are extremely powerful and are heard on the Throne of Grace.

It is so important that you do not compromise or water down your gifts. Today, perhaps more than ever, we need to have people stand up and be counted. I believe that the Lord is looking for people who are truly committed and "all in." It is critical that we're not lukewarm but "on fire" for the Lord and His will in our lives.

> Revelation 3: 15-16 "I know your works;
> I know that you are neither cold nor hot.
> I wish you were either cold or hot. So,
> because you are lukewarm, neither hot
> nor cold, I will spit you out of my
> mouth."

To be a new creation in Christ and get the stain of lack of forgiveness and sin out of your life, get out of your comfort zone. Expand your faith and spirituality by embracing new types of prayer or spiritual activities. If you haven't prayed the Divine Mercy Chaplet, begin praying it. You may think you are not a public speaker, but try volunteering to give a teaching at a prayer meeting or an organization you attend. Begin reading Scripture daily and memorize some verses and use them in conversation.

Instead of being part of the problem by holding onto hostility, be an encourager to those around you.

> 1 Thessalonians 5: 11,14 "Therefore encourage one another and build one another up, as indeed you do.
>
> "We urge you brothers, admonish the idle, clear the fainthearted, support the weak, be patient with all."

It is amazing that when you encourage others, your attitude toward others changes and it is much more difficult to hold onto animosity.

Also change your attitude towards yourself. Forgiveness often needs to start with ourselves.

Hebrews 3:13 "Encourage yourselves daily, while it is still 'today,' so that none of you may grow hardened by the deceit of sin."

So many times we find it difficult to forgive others because we see in them something we don't like about ourselves. Bless others with your love and prayers and you will be blessed beyond anything you can imagine. Forgiveness is accepting Jesus in your heart and embracing God's love and forgiving others by growing in Christ's love.

When we forgive others, we see them through the eyes of Jesus. We can better understand their brokenness and pain. We begin to accept them for who they are and separate their sin from who they are as a person.

Everything about forgiveness is accepting the love of Jesus into our hearts and souls. It is changing our hearts and souls so that we have compassion. Do not be afraid and do not fear! God is with you now and forever!

Examine yourself and ask yourself if you are resisting returning evil for evil or wanting to give some type of revenge, even in a subtle way. Do we truly want the best for people and pray for them and their welfare? Do we pray blessings on them, even when they have hurt us deeply? Do we come to their aid when they are down and out and need help or do we ignore them and think that they are getting what they deserve?

Let us never forget that forgiveness flows to us from Christ so that we may truly be instruments of His love and peace. To obtain the blessings and ultimately the salvation that God wants to give us, we must learn to say and practice Luke 23:34:

> "Father, forgive them, they know not what they do."

Forgiveness is the foundation of the power of the Cross. A forgiving heart connects us to the Sacred Heart of Jesus and His immense love and joy! I pray God's blessings on you and your loved ones in your pursuit of forgiveness.

CHAPTER 19
FINAL THOUGHTS AND PRAYER

During the course of this book, you have been challenged to change your behavior toward those whom you have not forgiven. It is critical to see them through the eyes of Christ, to love them unconditionally without judgment. We clearly have delineated that it is through the grace of Jesus, which is truly a miracle, that we are able to forgive.

Please reflect upon anyone with whom you have been angry for a period of time. It could be someone whom you have had a grudge against or feel bitter toward, or whom you haven't spoken to for a long period of time because of hostility or ill will. This could be relatives, loved ones, friends, co-workers, brothers, sisters, parents, aunts, cousins or anyone else for whom our lack of forgiveness might be blocking us from receiving God's great love and forgiveness.

Go to the Lord in prayer and then make a list of those whom you need to forgive. Ask the Lord to forgive you and give you the grace to forgive them unconditionally. It is important to pray to the Lord to change your heart so that it may conform to the Sacred Heart of Jesus. Ask our Blessed Mother to intercede for you. Pray for those who have hurt you and ask for their forgiveness through prayer or in person when led by the Lord.

In Scripture we are told over and over to bear with one another and forgive those who have hurt us.

> Ephesians 4: 31-32 "All bitterness, fury, anger, shouting, and reviling must be removed from you, along with all malice. [And] be kind to one another, compassionate, forgiving one another as God has forgiven you in Christ."

When we personify these words, our lives will change forever! After all, Jesus demonstrated to us the ultimate forgiveness by His words on the

Cross: "Father, forgive them, they know not what they do."

In our final thoughts, I offer you this prayer to be said aloud:

"Heavenly Father, I offer You all that I am and all that I have, body and soul. I surrender to You my past, present and future, with all my problems, habits, sins, medical issues, finances, job and relationships. I give You my health, family, marriage, children, grandchildren and friends.

I give You all of my hurt, pain, worry, doubt, fear and anxiety and I ask for Your healing love to wash over me and transform me into Your image. I release everything into Your compassionate and loving heart. Open my eyes to see You clearly, my ears to hear Your voice and direction and my heart to love You more deeply. I want to feel Your loving embrace now and forever.

Lord, open the doors that only You can open in my life and close the doors that need to be closed. Set my path directly to You. Create in me a clean heart that is pure of heart. Restore in me Your Spirit of forgiveness and mercy so that I may always forgive others and myself no matter what has occurred in the past or may occur in the future.

For the sake of Your precious love and sorrowful passion, I ask You to forgive all of my sins against You and Your children. Heal me of any sickness, addiction or disease which has entered my body that has been caused by sin in my life. Lord Jesus, forgive me of all my sins, whether they be known or unknown.

I am truly sorry for offending You due to my sins and lack of forgiveness. I repent of having false gods in my life that have replaced You. Please forgive me of not loving You with all my heart, mind, body and soul, disrespecting my body and not loving my neighbor.

Cover me with Your Precious Blood and surround me with Your holy heavenly angels to intercede for me. Let no areas of darkness remain in me, especially those areas in which I have not forgiven others or myself. Remove any addiction from me and transform my whole being with Your healing light and love.

Precious Jesus, I surrender to Your love and peace. I praise You for being the God of hope, love, mercy and forgiveness. Thank you for transforming me into Your agent of love, through the intercession of the Blessed Mother, the power of the Holy Spirit in Jesus' name. Amen.

God bless you and your family and loved ones, now and forever!

Deacon Steve Greco

ABOUT THE AUTHOR

Deacon **Steve Greco** is a dynamic speaker and author, and is founder of Spirit Filled Hearts Ministry. He is a man of vibrant faith with the charisms of healing and teaching rooted in his deep love and knowledge of the Word of God. His fatherly heart embraces each soul he touches with God's tender mercy and love.

Deacon Steve was ordained a permanent deacon for the Roman Catholic Diocese of Orange, California on May 17, 2007 and the bishop assigned him to St. Elizabeth Ann Seton Parish in Irvine. He worked as a healthcare executive for 35 years until retiring in 2016. In 2014, Our Lord moved Deacon Steve to found Spirit Filled Hearts Ministry in order to serve and spread the Good News of Jesus Christ. He delivers talks and leads healing services in California and throughout the United States in parishes and at conferences. He is host of "Empowered by the Spirit," his weekly radio program heard on Relevant Radio, 930AM and 1000AM, Sundays at 12 p.m. Pacific Time.

Deacon Steve has served on the boards of Obria, the SCRC Charismatic Renewal, the Loyola Institute for Spirituality and the Diocese of Orange Diaconate Formation. He has been married 47 years to wife Mary Anne, with whom he has three children and four grandchildren. He has published four other books: *365 Days of Praise, Reflections on the Holy Spirit, Expect and Experience Miracles* and *Overcoming Adversity Through Miracles.*

Spirit Filled Hearts Ministry travels internationally delivering Divine Mercy Conferences, seminars and parish missions and participating in special events; regular topics include "Life in the Spirit" seminars and "Empowered by the Spirit, Expect and Experience Miracles."

55766201R00139

Made in the USA
Middletown, DE
18 July 2019